THEODORE KOMISARJEVSKY

THEODORE KOMISARJEVSKY

MYSELF

AND

THE THEATRE

NEW YORK
E. P. DUTTON & CO., INC.

TO
DIDI

I cannot omit to thank here Lord and Lady Howard de Walden, Mr. and Mrs. Lee Mathews, Mr. Sidney Bernstein, Miss Lydia Sherwood, and Mr. H. Whitman for their friendly assistance to me while I was writing this book.

T. K.

Bloomsbury, London.
    August, 1929.

CONTENTS

CONTENTS

CONTENTS — *continued*

LIST OF ILLUSTRATIONS

LIST OF ILLUSTRATIONS—*continued*

Car tout ce que je raconte, je l'ai vu ; et si j'ai pu me tromper en le voyant, bien certainement je ne vous trompe point en vous le disant.

S<small>TENDHAL</small>.

CHAPTER ONE

A holiday abroad—Moscow during the Revolution—Work in the Moscow Theatres 1918-1919—An attack of nerves—My journey to the Polish frontier—Trials and Tribulations—Warsaw—I arrive in London

> All the blasted Moscow rooks
> Have revolution in their looks . . .

hummed the bearded izvoztchik, as he drove me on a hot July afternoon in 1919 at a snail's pace, across Moscow towards the railway station. I believe it was the only vehicle left in the town, as we did not meet another all the way along the desolate and dusty streets.

Strange as it may seem, since at the time all the doors of Revolutionary Russia were closed and exit was considered impossible, I was starting off with the intention of taking a holiday no nearer home than in Italy !

After the war years and strenuous work during the Revolution I needed one badly. I wanted to have a rest abroad not only becase of the trying conditions of life in Russia at that time, but because I longed to renew acquaintance with certain places in Western Europe, whose access had been denied me for six years, and where I had studied and spent my holidays before the war.   For Italy I had always had a special affection—

> Non so d'onde viene.
> Quel tenero affetto . . .

Probably because I was born there, although I was taken to Russia while still a small child.   The only thing that I was conscious of in those early days of my life in Italy was that opposite our house was an open air Theatre and that I used to listen on the balcony in the arms of my nurse to " Trovatore," " Un Ballo in Maschera " and other operas—at least so I was told by my mother.   Later however I used to go to Italy quite often to stay with my father, who lived there the last ten years of his life and was buried in Rome under the cypresses of the Testaccio quite near the tomb of Shelley.   He started his operatic career as an Italian singer under the assumed name of Di Pietro and even fought for Italy in the Legions of Garibaldi.

My last winter in Moscow (1918-19) had been what would seem to a Londoner "living hell," but to us after several years of such conditions, more or less normal.

At night both streets and houses with smashed windows and empty shops were in complete darkness, as there was no longer electricity or gas except in government buildings and different public institutions. Lamp oil or candles could be got only for a fortune.   No private shops were open and there was no proper food to be had, even on ration cards.   On special days after hours of queuing at the rare government shops a salted herring, some dried peas or perhaps a black biscuit, tasting like sawdust and stale beetroot, were supplied as food for a whole family. Very often instead of tea people drank a liquid made of grilled carrots. Such things as a steak of horse flesh, sugar, butter or soap were considered great luxuries, only to be obtained at profiteering prices in mysterious places unknown to the Cheka. A pound of butter, for instance, cost the equivalent of the maximum weekly salary paid at that time by the Soviet Government to its Officials ; a sack of flour cost about £10 and a glass of real coffee with milk about £1.

There was no fuel with which to heat the house. The drain, water and heating pipes were frozen—the frost sometimes reached 40 deg. C. below zero. The inhabitants of a house lived as a rule in one room, in the middle of which they sat, like Esquimos, round a small brick stove, which they were obliged to make themselves. To keep these stoves going they made use of the furniture, and even doors were taken off their hinges.

The clothes worn by Moscovites at that time would be too extreme even for an English musical comedy tramp, and shoes without holes were a rare luxury. Some people wore sandals made of the bark of trees or cardboard.

There is no need to remark that during that winter there were no such things as taxis (A taxi ! What a joke !) and izvoztchiks (horse-cabs) were very seldom seen. A few electric trams were running, but these were so overcrowded that people had to hang on to the outsides. Travelling in these trams was little better than suicide as the passengers were swarming with lice which were carriers of typhus germs, from which thousands of people in Moscow died.

Even the corpses of Russian citizens could not find peace, as there was no time to dig graves and make coffins for all of them. One night a friend of my servant—(as one was not allowed to have servants, the woman was known as my aunt)—came to visit her and died suddenly in her bed. I could not get him moved for two days, and only through the intervention of a high government official was he eventually taken away wrapped in a blanket, to be buried in a common grave.

The perpetual fear however, for one's very existence, made all these inconveniences seem comparatively trivial. The country was full of Cheka spies—even one's own brother was not above suspicion—(though I did not suspect mine)—and these spies were always ready to condemn the most innocent action as a crime against the Revolution, the inevitable punishment for which was death. At night, people listened to every sound that broke the silence in the street outside, dreading to hear the rumble of a motor-van, as it was in these vehicles that officials of the Cheka arrived to arrest the citizens. One night they came to search the flat of a friend of mine, but finding nothing —(he never knew what they were looking for)—they entered the flat next door, arrested the man living there and shot him in the courtyard under my friend's windows.   His body was still lying in the snow when my friend left the following morning to take a rehearsal at his Theatre.

It may well seem strange that in such circumstances the theatres were still open.

During the first years of the Revolution in the centre of Moscow alone there were two Opera and Ballet Theatres, about twelve dramatic repertory theatres, one Operetta (or Musical Comedy) Theatre in addition to various Studios and Theatrical Schools.

All these were well patronised by the new public, and most of them were full at every performance. This was not because there was plenty of light in the auditoriums, or because there were comfortable stalls in which to sit, or because the people were merely looking for amusement.   The " grey public," as the masses were called in Russia before the Revolution, went to the Theatre, because it was an entertaining form of education for them.   Indeed, is not the Theatre, where ideas are presented in an imaginative, emotional form, the most powerful means by which to influence the masses ?   Lenin who understood the power of the Theatre said that in a Communist State " it should be *closely* associated with the Proletariat . . . and should make its appeal to the millions of workers, who represent the hope of the country, its force and its future."   The Russian Theatre has always retained the status originally given to it by the Empress Catherine the Second, who called it " The School of the People."   The Russian

revolutionaries have not forgotten that the Theatre
played a very important part in preparing the Great
French Revolution, that it hastened the downfall of
the old institutions, and like their French predecessors
they consider the Theatre " the most active and direct
medium to arm human reason with invincible
strength."

Outside Russia very little is known about the
Russian Theatre from the beginning of the Soviet
regime in 1917 until 1920.   Nothing has been written
about the work of the first Soviet Theatre (the Moscow
Soviet Opera House), the small district Soviet Theatres
in Moscow, the Soviet Theatres in the Provinces, the
artistic and educational Union of Workers' Organisations, and very little about the first years of the
" Proletcult," of the experiments of one of the best,
but at the same time one of the most modest advanced
producers, E. Vachtangov, and of other humble, but
nevertheless important workers in the so-called
" proletarian " theatre in Russia. All the new
principles of acting and producing, which were
adopted in our theatres after 1920, and of which so
much has been written abroad, were laid down during
the first years of the Soviet regime.   " Constructive "
(cubistic or skeleton) sets, " bio-mechanical " acting
—all these have been seen since 1917 in the pieces
produced by the " Proletcult " in its principal House,
a former millionaire's palace, by some of the district
Theatres, by the Moscow Soviet Opera House (in
my productions of " Lohengrin," " The Barber of

CHESTERTON'S "THE MAN WHO WAS THURSDAY." MOSCOW, 1924. Tairov.

Seville," "Fidelio," etc., and in A. Tairov's outstanding production of A. Rubinstein's "Demon "),
by the Union of the Workers' Organizations, etc.

While working in the Theatre in Russia during the
Revolution, one felt its importance for the life of the
Nation, and this gave the enthusiasm to work and
the strength to endure the prevailing hardships and
difficulties.

To remain at the head of a Theatre during the first
years of the Revolution meant not only managing the
Theatre and producing plays, but fighting hard for
one's ideas and for the existence of everyone working
in the Theatre.

In addition to managing and producing in my own
repertory Theatre (patronized since 1918 by the aforementioned Union of the Workers' Organizations),
I directed from 1917 the productions at the Soviet
Opera House and in 1918 was elected Managing
Director and Producer of the Moscow Grand State
Theatre of Opera and Ballet. I was producing in
both the latter Theatres before the Revolution, having
left the second (which was then the Imperial Grand
Opera Theatre) to work in the first, which was known
at the time as the Moscow Ziminne Private Opera,
where I remained when it was taken over by the
Soviets.

In my own Theatre alone I produced ten plays during
the winter of 1918–19 :—" Il Seraglio " by Mozart ;
" Le Mariage Forcé " by Molière ; " Haensel and
Gretel " by Humperdinck ; " Le Mariage de Figaro "

by Beaumarchais; Shakespeare's " The Merry Wives of Windsor " (with music by Nicolai) and " The Tempest " (with music by Arensky); " The Tales of Hoffman " by Offenbach; " Mozart and Salieri " by Rimsky Korsakov; Leoncavallo's " Pagliacci "; and " Androcles and the Lion " by G. B. Shaw. It may seem strange to the reader, that the repertoire of my Theatre included plays as well as operas. The idea behind all my productions was to create a *synthetic* Theatre, about which I speak later, where all forms of art could be harmoniously united in one single show. I introduced music into the plays, rewrote the librettos of the operas to suit the character and the rhythm of the music, and inserted dialogues and speaking parts in the operas. Hence the singers took part in the plays as well as the operas, and similarly, the dramatic actors took part in the operas.

I was teaching at a School of Acting, which I had founded (in 1910) myself, giving lectures at one of the Universities, writing articles, designing scenery and costumes, and attending innumerable meetings in defence of my theatrical productions. I never went to bed before four or five in the morning and very often spent all night working or conferring with people who were otherwise occupied during the day. I had to run from one institution to another at opposite ends of the town (Moscow is an enormous place, built like Rome on seven hills) to get food, lodgings, travelling permits, etc. for my actors, stage hands and other employees, and even stockings for the wife of one actor and milk for the new born baby of another.

I must here pay a tribute to my chief, the government commissar of all the Moscow Theatres, E. K. Malinovskaya. This dear elderly lady—who was a friend of Lenin, and was called by Maxim Gorky, another friend of hers, " the stone woman "—was a great help to me in the stress of those times. It was largely due to her energy and self-sacrificing love for the Theatre and those who worked for it that the standard of the productions in the Moscow Theatres after the Revolution was so high and that the former Imperial Theatres—called by certain political groups bourgeois institutions—survived (although I personally thought that a good shaking would not have been a bad thing for those strongholds of intrigues and conceit), and that quite a number of artistes escaped starvation or even a worse fate. She always had free access to Lenin, and through her insistence on one occasion he interrupted an important meeting of the Peoples Commissars (Secretaries of State) at two o'clock in the morning to receive a theatrical deputation which came to petition him not to sign the decree of " nationalisation of actors." (Lenin, by the way, granted their request and abandoned the measure)

The difficulties under which actors and other artists had to work were enormous. We were often obliged to heat the theatre ourselves by filling and lighting the boilers in the basements, and even then there was usually snow on the mirrors in the large foyer, where the pupils of my school (it was in the same building as my Theatre) had ballet lessons, dancing bare legged and bare armed. Frequently during performances the breath of the singers on the stage was visible in such clouds of vapour that they called themselves samovars. A pianist once played in the Concert Hall of the former Club of the Nobility in knitted gloves and had to stop playing as one of his fingers had frozen. I remember seeing the operatic womens' choir, representing nymphs, in snow boots. A violinist of the Grand State Theatre Orchestra fell off his chair during a performance because he had not eaten for days. One morning when a young actress of my Theatre did not turn up to rehearsal we discovered that she had died of typhus during the night alone in a freezing room—and that she must have been ill for days without mentioning it. A scenery designer suddenly and mysteriously disappeared, and we were told later that as a former Imperial officer and involved in some conspiracy he had been secretly arrested and shot during the night by the Cheka. One of the greatest character actresses in Russia, O. O. Sadovskaya, died of vermin.

The salaries paid in the Theatres were quite impossible to live on, and actors were obliged to do other work to supplement their incomes, which gave rise to further difficulties. One night, owing to the fact that they were earning money elsewhere, the whole male choir of the Soviet Opera was absent from the first act of Rimsky-Korsakov's " Coq d'Or " and

King Dodon had to address empty benches with a stage manager, impersonating the whole crowd, instead of a large assembly of courtiers.

How to get canvas, wood, paint, and other materials for scenery and costumes was a great problem. At one time scenery paint could only be obtained from some profiteering Chinamen, but as the Theatres were owned by the State, and profiteering was a crime, it was impossible to patronise these people. Fortunately, every Russian Theatre, especially those under the former Imperial management, had a large stock of scenery and costumes, and whenever possible, we adapted these to our needs.

Perhaps the most trying thing in the working life of a theatrical director during the Revolution was his relationship with certain committees, consisting of representative theatrical employees. These committees existed in every Theatre and attempted to organise them on socialistic lines, and were usually entirely ignorant of how to run a Theatre. Eventually the Soviets realised the incompetence and inefficiency of these committees and gave more freedom and scope to the initiative of individuals. At first however, these committees were elected at a general meeting of the entire staff of a Theatre and possessed great power. In the Soviet Opera House my activities as Director were controlled by a body consisting of a cloak-room attendant, a cleaner, a cellist, a conductor (and not a very good one), a second-rate mezzo soprano, a property master, etc. When I dared to protest against their decisions as to which operas I should produce and to whom I should assign the parts, they replied that I was " not worthy to direct a Theatre in a Bolshevik country, being of a noble family," which resulted in my leaving the theatre. However, after a fortnight's absence some delegates from the company came to my flat and begged me to return as the committee were unable to carry on.

These people on committees were often typical of the thousands of opportunists and adventurers from every class of the Russian people, who were shown up in their true colours by the Revolution. They were clever enough to influence the masses by dint of shouting and stirring their lower instincts and were elected into every organisation—some even holding important offices—until circumstances proved their hypocrisy. They had no convictions of their own and were alternatively for Bolshevism, Tsarism, or anything else which they thought might be profitable. These creatures were not only a hindrance elsewhere, but were responsible for a great many of the horrors of the Revolution.

I hope that these details about life in Moscow during the Revolution may suffice to enable my readers to understand that it was not so very remarkable that when I woke one morning I was seized with a violent attack of nerves. It was really the beginning of a kind of a mania persecutionis, which later developed in a mild form until it seemed to me while walking in the streets that somebody was following me or while

RUSSIAN " PROPAGANDA " THEATRICAL POSTER

lying in bed wide awake at night that somebody was knocking at the door or trying to break in.

The sun shone brightly through the window of my bedroom and suddenly I saw myself in 1913, a carefree lazzarone, lying on the beach of Sestri Levante and breakfasting on a lemon, a piece of bread and a fiasco of Chianti warm from the sun. Stretched in my bed I thought of fairy Viennese and Parisian cafés. They had always had a great attraction for me. For one who like myself often wishes to be amongst people without having to speak to them, there is no better place than a café. To sit on a " térrace " of a café is just as interesting, perhaps even more so than being a spectator in a Theatre, and it certainly costs much less. I confess with shame, that I was imagining mountains of pastries, sacher and linzer torten, apéritifs, brioches. I saw gay, well dressed men and women sitting in the cafés, and dreamt of driving in cars or strolling along the boulevards without the necessity of a special permit to do so or of running the risk of being arrested and shot. Seized by an irresistible urge I dressed hastily and ran to every possible organisation in an effort to get permission to go to Italy for three months.

I will not describe all the difficulties I had in obtaining what was well-nigh impossible. Nobody at that time, except on very urgent business, was allowed even to travel by rail. It took me over a month to get a permit, and even then it was only to go as far as Minsk to visit a friend; I chose that town, not because I had a friend there, but because the trains from Moscow in the direction of the Polish frontier were not running beyond Minsk. I left the problem of getting to Italy to be settled on my arrival at Minsk.

The journey from Moscow, which took about twelve hours before the Revolution, lasted forty on this occasion, and instead of lolling in a " bourgeois " sleeper I had to sit in a bus-like third class carriage with broken windows and smashed doors. The train was so overcrowded, mostly with discharged soldiers from the Moscow hospitals, that I could not leave my seat without treading on bodies lying on the floor of my carriage.

As there were no ordinary trains going further than Minsk, I had to continue my journey thence in a cattle wagon with some workers who were on their way to pull up the railway track beyond the frontier station. These comrades whom I had discovered at Minsk had at first refused to allow me to accompany them, calling me a " mangey bourgeois," but when I offered them some eucalyptus pastilles—a whole box of which they promptly consumed—they hoisted me into the truck still calling me different untranslatable names, just as the train, which consisted of our wagon and a heavily puffing engine, started to move. Without abusing the courtesy of my companions I must add that my seat was scarcely a comfortable one, as I was sitting on the floor in the open doorway of the truck with my legs dangling over the wheels outside. Jogging along, I gazed out over the spacious peaceful countryside so typically Russian with the calmness of colour, and so unlike the average English conception derived from fierce-coloured theatrical representations. Pale green fields of high corn, goldish from the morning sun, mauve-brown stretches of forests on the far away horizon changed into thin woods of gay white " curly " birches or into shadowy forests of fir trees ; from time to time the train passed the wooden hut of a signal-man outside which he, or a woman wearing a kerchief over her head, a waistless blouse and a skirt, all of some nondescript colours, stood like barefooted sentries holding the signal flag. The tender blue sky flecked with white clouds, which in our childhood we used to call " little lambs," seemed transparent and endlessly wide. Against those boundless skies of Russia the earth itself seems small and insignificant and there is little wonder that the Russian feels the presence of God, dwelling there above in the vast blue infinity.

After about an hour's journey the train stopped at a platform surrounded by fields. There was no station building near it, nor any houses, and only far away from the line could one distinguish a few straw roofs of some crooked huts looking as though they had grown into the earth, and a small pink church with a belfry. A couple of armed Cheka officials came aboard ; they searched me, relieved me of some of my money, though it was carefully concealed in my shoes, the lining of my coat etc., and the train moved on again. At the next halt right in the middle of a forest we heard the engine driver shouting for us.   On descending we were informed by him—as he chewed roasted seeds and spat the husks all over the place— that there was no more fuel on the engine, and that " if the comrades were very keen on finishing their journey, they had better run and fetch some wood from the forest."   After a couple of hours of wood chopping and loading the engine, the train started again and a couple of hours later in the afternoon, I reached the Western frontier of Russia, a low wooden station, just as the Soviets were evacuating it in face of the advancing Polish army.

On being thrown out on the platform by the comrades I was promptly arrested by a heavily armed official of the local Cheka, who, after ruthlessly searching me in an empty ticket office, relieved me of nearly all the money I had left and dealt a fatal blow to my prospects of going to Italy.   He took even my watch and a bottle of eau de cologne.   On my asking to be allowed to keep the latter on the plea that I needed it for washing purposes—as there was no water on the trains—he retorted :—" Why should *you* wash, when the Red army goes about unwashed ? " With this remark, he flung me back on the platform, advising me to stay there until he gave me permission to leave.   .

Sitting there for a couple of hours afforded me plenty of opportunity to speculate on my future, which had suddenly become very uncertain !

On my right was Russia and my past life including

thirteen years theatrical work. (Thirteen—a fatal number in my life). On my left, somewhere beyond those plains and stretches of forest, lay western Europe, which up till then I had known merely as a region in which to spend a pleasant holiday or to study, and not as a place in which to work for a living, although years previously when strolling along the Paris boulevards the large multi-coloured theatrical posters (the Russian State Theatres posters were small and innocently pale) had appeared to me very attractive. How deceptive they proved to be later !

As the sun sank—a large red disc—behind the distant forests—it seemed like a danger signal, warning me of the West—and I decided to go back to Moscow.

It was just at that moment that I saw my friend of the local Cheka and others running along the platform towards a train standing some distance up the line, shouting that the Polish army was surrounding the district from the East. I hurried after them, but on attempting to enter one of the dilapidated carriages I was pushed off and fell on the line. The train steamed away, and I was left to my fate.

However I soon had reason to be grateful for this lack of courtesy when I heard that this very train was destroyed later by Polish bombing aeroplanes.

There now remained nothing but to get a conveyance to take me anywhere, and I made my way to the village where at nightfall I found an old peasant about to drive his cart to the Polish frontier six miles

c

away.   He agreed to take me with him for the large sum of 500 roubles (about £5 then).   Although he called me " comrade." he insisted on being paid—not in Soviet money—but in notes of the Tsarist regime.

I need not tell here of my various adventures during the short journey to Warsaw which was made very long for me by the different arrests, threats of execution and internment camps, etc.   Suffice to say that one evening completely worn out, with a beard of a few days growth, and accompanied by various unpleasant insects I found myself in Warsaw in a comfortable hotel room, with a bath and even a large cake of soap. This room according to the Moscow laws would have been considered more than large enough for two families to live in.   The next morning, as I had decided to look for a job in Paris, I went to the French Consulate to get a visa, but much to my surprise was informed that for Russians the happy pre-war times had passed and that whoever we were—" White," or " Red," or " Green " or " colourless," we could not now be admitted to any country in the whole world without a special personal permit.   Of course I applied for such a permit at once, but had to wait endless weeks for it to come from France.   I re-member that every night during that forced stay in Warsaw I used to look for shooting stars.   Some kind friend of mine advised me to do so ; he told me, that if I could see twelve stars fall in succession my wish would certainly come true, i.e., the permit would arrive. I tried very hard to achieve this feat but in vain.

However, on the morning after the thirty-eighth night of my astronomical or astrological experiments or whatever they could be called, the blessed permit arrived and I was even given a seat in the " diplomatic train," which took me to Paris. I did not look for a job there that time, because S. Diaghileff, one of the kindest and most energetic men I ever knew, advised me to go to London. I reached Waterloo Station on a cold rainy morning two months after I left Moscow, with my last ten shillings in my pocket.

After four lonely weeks in London, of which I have now grown very fond, I was asked, through Albert Coates, who had been for some time the conductor of the Petersburg Imperial Opera House, to produce some operas which led to subsequent engagements in London, Paris and New York and through which I made my first acquaintance with the *commercial* Theatre, an institution quite unknown in Russia.

CHAPTER TWO

The Russian Imperial Theatres—Ex-Colonel Director—The "pillars"—Imperial Stage Directors—The Press—The Theatre as money-maker and as art—Aims and Finance of Imperial Theatres—Private Theatre Directors—Cabotinage on the "commercial" stage—Speculation in rents—Conditions for artistic Theatres—Commercial managements and "backers"

THE last Director of the five Russian Imperial Theatres*—which were considered as regards acting, singing and dancing "exemplary" Theatres in Russia —was such a small man physically that he seemed quite lost when sitting at the big desk in the vastness of his study in Theatre Street. This street was one of the most attractive in Petersburg, quite short, a long Empire building on each side, ochre-yellow in colour with white columns and ornaments. At one

---

* V. A. Teliakovsky was Director of the Imperial Theatres from 1901 until the Revolution of 1917. These Theatres are indebted to him for the modern—and higher—standard of productions. The producers and conductors, Sanin, Fokin, Meyerhold, myself, Rachmaninov, Albert Coates, Emile Cooper, were engaged by him. It was under his régime that Pavlova, Kouznetzova, Karsavina, Lopokova, Nijinsky, Mordkin, L. Novikov, and Chaliapin became known. He introduced work by modern writers and musicians into the repertoire and was the first to engage for the Imperial Theatres designers of scenery of such recognised merit as Anisfeld, Bakst, Alexander Benois, A. Golovin, K. Korovin.

The five Imperial Theatres—three of which were in Petersburg and two in Moscow—had seven permanent companies of actors.

end of it stood the Alexandra Imperial Theatre, built at the beginning of the XIXth century, as was the street itself, by the Italian architect Rossi.   Although a former colonel of Horse Guards, the Director looked more like a bank clerk than a soldier, the only military thing about his appearance being his pointed moustache.   I could never imagine him on horseback, nor was it thought that he would make an efficient Director when he was appointed by the Minister of the Court, Baron (later Count) Frederiks, his step father and the former commander of his regiment.   Still, he proved a success, and was, like C. B. Cochran in London or Reinhardt in Germany, that rare combination, a sound business man who possessed artistic ideas.

It is strange but true that for many years those who have done most for the Theatre as an art, and have encouraged new ideas on the stage have begun as amateurs.   Among the latter we can name Antoine, the Duke George II of Meiningen, Stanislavsky, Diaghileff,

---

These were : two Ballet Companies, including soloists and corps de ballet, two operatic companies, three dramatic companies (two Russian and one French).   Besides these the Imperial Theatres had seven Symphony Orchestras, two Brass Bands, two Choirs, two Theatrical Academies with Ballet and Dramatic Sections, a large library, a Theatrical and Art periodical, workshops for providing scenery, properties, costumes, etc.   This enormous organisation gradually grew out of a small Court Theatre called the Hermitage Theatre, built in the year 1789 by the celebrated architect Guarenghi, on the spot where the Old Winter Palace stood in which Peter the Great died.   All the foregoing theatres are to-day supported by the Soviet Government.

Vera Komisarjevsky, Gordon Craig, Coppeau, and the founders of The New York Theatre Guild. We need not, however, conclude from this that professionals have done nothing progressive for the Theatre, though it remains a fact that the big move ments in the art of the Theatre of late years have been initiated by non-professional people. This seems to be mainly due to the fact that " trained " actors are usually only capable of visualising the Theatre and its possibilities from their own narrow point of view, i.e., from the stage itself, and therefore often fail to grasp the significance of the Theatre as a whole. On the other hand, those who are not trained in any one particular branch of theatrical work, i.e., intelligent amateurs of the Theatre—as observers from the front —attain a much broader attitude towards the Theatre in all its aspects.

The diminutive colonel who controlled the Imperial Theatres until the Revolution was himself an intelligent and talented amateur to whom Russian art is greatly indebted.

It was no easy job to manage the huge organisation of those Theatres, especially for a man like the Colonel who had " revolutionary " ideas about the stage. The Director of the Imperial Theatres had to keep in contact with the Court, with the various members of the Imperial family, and with all the high government officials. As may be imagined, these circles were very conservative and all of them had something to say concerning the management of the Theatres belonging

to the Crown. But the most difficult task of a
Director lay in dealing with actors and artists of big
reputations who had held their engagements from the
Crown for ten to twenty or more years and considered
themselves veritable " pillars of the Imperial Stage."
These people were convinced, and their opinion was
shared by numberless influential people and the
conservative press, that the Imperial Theatres must
collapse the moment they ceased to play the leading
roles. Prince Serge Volkonsky, a man with exquisite
artistic taste, who had preceded the colonel as Director,
had lost his appointment after eighteen months because
he had been too straight-forward and not sufficiently
hypocritical to refrain from quarrelling with some of
these pillars. The Director, before Volkonsky, had
kept his job for a very long time only because he had
let everybody interfere in the management of the
Imperial Theatres, and had ignored the lazy, egotistical
routine which had caused the state of stagnation in the
Theatres and with which the diminutive colonel had
to cope. In order to be able to produce interesting
plays which to the Court officials and especially to the
pillars seemed " unusual " and " degenerate," or to
engage new leading actors, modern producers or
scenic artists, the colonel had to use very ingenious
tactics and had an endless struggle against the caprices
and intrigues of nearly everybody around him, and
very often had to put up with quite wild demands from
the leading actors and actressess. For instance there
was among the pillars a prima ballerina who, (living at

the time with a Grand Duke, and previously with Nicholas the Second himself) unofficially managed the whole Petersburg Imperial Ballet and dictated which ballets the Director should produce for her, the dates of production, and even went so far as to insist that no other prima ballerina should appear in these ballets. In the Petersburg Alexandra Dramatic Theatre another unofficial Director, the leading actress Marie Savina, called by the leading comedian " Marya the warrior " reigned supreme.   At the time of the colonel's appointment she had been acting there for nearly thirty years.   In addition to excessive cunning this lady had a poisonous sense of humour and a vile temper, but happened to be an exceptionally good actress and to possess an influential husband.   In face of these " assets " the Director had to do, or at least make a pretence of doing, whatever she wanted.   The colonel had to submit the season's repertoire at the Alexandra Theatre for her approval before he was allowed to make any decisions.

On one occasion at rehearsal, a new producer—a temperamental Armenian—was so enraged by Savina's provocative behaviour that he flung a lamp at her, shouting :

—For thirty years everyone in this Theatre has been living under the tyranny of that woman's skirts and not a single man has had the pluck to say he's sick of it !

Fortunately for the colonel's plans, Savina confined her attention to those plays in which she herself

"The Merry Wives of Windsor," Moscow, 1918. Komisarjevsky.

acted and to those actresses of whom she was jealous,
which made it just possible for the poor man to carry
on his work in the Theatre, though he only succeeded
at the cost of continual sacrifices to her and others like
her. One of these sacrifices was my sister Vera
Komisarjevsky whose resignation from the Alexandra
Theatre he accepted when she was at the zenith of her
career.

Another of these dictators was a singer in the
Imperial operatic company—a first rate artist of world
fame—who not only chose his own parts and the
entire casts of the operas in which he sang, but also
the producers, conductors and scenic designers.
This man even had ridiculous clauses inserted in his
contracts with regard to such matters as complimentary seats to relations and friends, the free use of
costumes belonging to the Imperial Theatres for his
private tours, the right to absent himself during the
Season whenever he wished, etc. He was notorious
for having terrific rows at rehearsals and even during
performances, mostly with producers and conductors,
and frequently left the Theatre in a rage in the middle
of a show, until at last scarcely a single one out of a
dozen conductors remained who would conduct the
operas in which this famous artist sang. He had a
lively imagination in the matter of abusive language :
on the stage he once called the women's choir " Tyro-
lean cows " and on the occasion of a row with an old
Stage Director he shouted that the whole crowd of
producers of the Imperial Theatres were a lot of

" mangey Turkish hacks ! "   The fact that this singer and those conductors, producers, actors and artists who had to work with him did not throw up their work in the Imperial Theatres was entirely due to the energy and tact of the colonel Director.

The engagement of producers and modern artists to design the sets gave the pillars of the Imperial Theatres most cause for alarm.   They declared that " the work of the painters and producers was killing and nullifying the work of the actors," that " they knew what acting was, and didn't need lessons from degenerates and ignorant amateurs."

Until the end of the XIXth century there was no such person as a real producer in the Imperial Drama and Opera.   The pieces were staged by the actors themselves under the supervision of a Stage Director (Chief Régisseur) whose real interest lay more in the administrative side of the Theatre than in the business of putting on the plays.   A Stage Director was usally promoted to that post from that of Prompter or Stage Manager, as in the Army a colonel is promoted to the rank of general for long and zealous service. Eventually leading actors began to produce plays themselves which led to the engagement of special producers, an example which was set by the great Russian producer Stanislavsky in his Moscow Art Theatre.

Another source of obstruction which the colonel had to contend with was the press.   One influential musical critic, M. M. Ivanov, who was nevertheless a bad musician, never ceased his attacks on the Director for his "nauseating international taste in art." According to him the Imperial Theatres, instead of patronising "national" Russian music and Russian artists were producing "foreign cacophony and muck by Wagner, Debussy, and Richard Strauss" and "employing numerous foreigners." By numerous foreigners he meant such artists as the Chekoslovakian conductors Napravnik and Suk, the Englishman Albert Coates, the singers Felia Litvinne, Medea Figner, the dancers Grimaldi, Ferrero, Zambelli etc. Fortunately for the Director's career these accusations were only too obviously hysterical lies. The Imperial Theatres, at the time were producing, besides "foreign muck," the work of all the best Russian composers and writers and were employing hundreds of "national" Russian artists. Apart from that, xenophobia is not a characteristic Russian trait and neither the Court nor the public (with the exception of a small political party called "The Union of the True Russian People" famous for arranging Jewish "pogroms") regarded the art of the Theatre from Ivanov's point of view. As a matter of fact the high standard of Russian theatrical art was to a great extent directly due to its international outlook. The Imperial Ballet reached a level of perfection far exceeding that of any other Ballet in the World, not alone as the result of the work of Russian Ballet-masters like Gorsky and Fokin, but also from that of foreigners such as Marius Petipa, Johanson, Mendes, Helzer, and Enrico Cecchetti, who were

retained permanently as ballet-masters or teachers at
the Imperial Theatres. The high standard of the
musical side of the Petersburg Opera, the development of its orchestra into one of the best in the world,
was achieved by the Chekoslovakian Conductor
Edward Napravnik, who held his engagement there
for fifty years.

The evolution of the arts of acting and producing in
the Russian Theatres is largely due to the fact that our
theatrical artists are in permanent contact with the
western European Theatre without being afraid of its
influence. Before the Revolution the public ap-
preciated foreign plays, and the work of the foreigners
in the Theatre in general, every bit as much as that of
Russians. The late Serge Diaghileff achieved brilliant
results with his Russian Ballet (which had a widespread, although superficial, influence not only on
the British Theatre, but also on British painting and
music) because he sought and found inspiration, not
from a narrow " national " outlook but from the four
corners of the world. His dancers, as well as his
authors, scenic designers and conductors were of
various nationalities, and his enterprise as a whole was
a synthesis of international art—like the Imperial Ballet
—welded together by the genius of a Russian. The
same applies to Nikita Balieff's " Chauve Souris," so
well known in western Europe. This type of show
described in Germany as " Klein-Kûnst " Theatre is by
no means a truly " national " Russian entertainment as
is generally imagined in England and America. Al-

though inspiration for most of his settings was derived from the primitive grotesque art of the Russian peasants (Koustari), from their home-made bright-coloured toys, jugs, coloured prints etc., and from byzantine ikons, Balieff's whole idea of his theatre was taken from western Europe, from the French and German " cabarets," and in quite a number of his most popular items (*e.g.* "Katinka," "The Wooden Soldiers," "The Three Huntsmen," etc.) he has made use of German or French music. " The Chauve Souris " in fact like Diaghileff's Ballet is another example of an artistic enterprise in which the inspiration of a Russian artist has blended Russian ideas with those of other countries.

The patriotic critic Ivanov, besides being an adherent to the " noble " ideas of the Union of the True Russians, bore a personal grudge against the new Director because the latter had refused to produce any of Ivanov's operas after one had failed in the Moscow Grand Theatre. Although the composer received no less than ten wreaths at the fall of the curtain on the first night of his chef d'oeuvre—all of them, by the way, sent by his Petersburg friends who did *not* hear his music—the opera ran for one night only. A few weeks later when Rimsky-Korsakov produced his new Opera " The Night of Christmas Eve " at the same Theatre, he was the recipient of but one modest laurel wreath and on being asked why he got so few and Ivanov so many, the great composer replied in his nasal voice :

—Because *I* am only a *composer* and *he* is a *critic !*

With few exceptions the Petersburg and Moscow critics of what would be called in England highbrow papers were no more kindly disposed to the Director than Ivanov, although they bore him no personal grudge. Some of them freely called him "a cavalry officer, who ought to be looking after horses and not Theatres," a "perverse ignoramus," etc.

"It might seem"—wrote the colonel years later in his *Memoires*—"mere nonsense to say that the press always praises what is bad and abuses everything good, nevertheless in most cases it is the truth. Theatrical critics only begin to praise good work when their opinion is no longer required and the public itself has solved the problem and pronounced its own verdict. The press is no use to anyone, either to the Theatre as an institution, artists, management, or the public."

In spite of his many enemies and their intrigues, the shrewd and gifted ex-colonel of Horse Guards succeeded in modernising the Imperial Theatres and in remaining Director for seventeen years. In May, 1917, however, he was dismissed for no other reasons than that (1) after the Revolution the actors in his Theatres took it into their heads to run things themselves and (2) the new Prince Lvov and Kerensky Governments had no wish to have an Imperial officer at the head of Republican Theatres. But the communal rule very soon proved unsuccessful, and the next Government, the Soviet, instead of retaining one single Director for all the former Imperial Theatres,

"The Tales of Hoffman." Doctor Daperutto's aria in the second act. Moscow, 1919. Komisarjevsky.

made the actors elect a Director for each of them, over every one of which a government Commissar was appointed, which by the way made life no easier for anybody. As for the one-time colonel of Horse Guards, he died in misery a few years later forgotten by nearly everyone.

I mention him here not only because, like Diaghileff and Vera Komisarjevsky, he could not be overlooked when speaking of modern art in the Russian Theatre, but because he often said : " The Theatre is not the place to make money, though there is no reason why it should not yield a certain profit. The man who runs a Theatre and whose main object is money-making is not an artist and does not understand the nature of the Theatre."

And that is neither more nor less than the plain truth. The artist must do what he sincerely wants to do, otherwise his work has neither meaning nor value. He is fortunate if his generation accepts him ; he is unlucky if it does not. His failure to please is by no means an indication of the quality of his work, but often merely a sign of the lack of understanding and the limited æsthetic taste of the public. Mr. G. B. Shaw at the age of thirty-seven was considered quite well off on, I believe, something like £7 a week, and Cézanne in his lifetime sold his pictures for 5 Francs apiece. Even if the public preferred Henry Irving in melodrama, he was justified in doing what he wanted to do as an artist—i.e. to act in Shakespeare—although the public did not patronise

Shakespeare in his day any more than it did before him or has since. We read that as early as the XVIIth century one had to look hard for a Theatre in London which gave " something more than rubbish " and that even the rare productions of Shakespeare's plays at that time were played to half empty houses. Two centuries later, to induce the London public to see Macready in " Othello " and " Romeo and Juliet," the management of the Drury Lane Theatre had to advertise in large letters " A Grand Dirge in Act V " of the latter play and added the note " concluding both performances with Grand Melo-Dramas." Similarly, in order to make the production of " The Merchant of Venice," in which Mr. Phelps played, sufficiently attractive to the public, they had to include " Magnificent scenery illustrating the Carnival of Venice." When I arrived in London in 1919 and asked to see some *good* modern *English* productions of plays by the greatest English poet, I was taken first to the Court Theatre which seemed to me then a mere suburban house, and witnessed " The Merchant of Venice " with Shylock played by a foreign actor. Later I was taken still further from the West End, and saw a production of a tragedy by Shakespeare which could only be described as a provincial helter skelter.

It is fortunate for dramatists that their work remains alive to be judged on its own merits after they themselves are dead, but it is a tragedy for an actor that his work lives only with himself. Very few people to-day remember Janet Achurch, although she was

one of the best actresses of the English Stage. Unfortunately for her commercial career, she acted in the
plays of Shaw and Ibsen which the artist in her liked
but the public of the eighteen-nineties did not. On
one occasion at the end of " A Dolls House, " when,
as Nora she had made her final exit and Helmer says
" She is gone ! " a woman in the audience loudly
exclaimed " So's my blasted money ! "

The ephemeral nature of the actor's art is in strong
contrast with the immortality of art itself. The eyes of
an artist see life in its entirety whereas the man in the
street is never able to see the forest for the trees. The
artist has visions of what is hidden beyond the foggy
horizon of material reality, whereas the average man
is conscious of little beyond his nose. The greater
the work of an artist, the less likely it is to be accepted
by the crowd, who can appreciate what is new in art
only after they have grown accustomed to it, and that
requires time. The flame of genius is too intense for
the general public, who, remaining slavishly true to
the old forms, find it irritating and inevitably adopt an
attitude of condemnation. An actor who is an artist
must be prepared to fight against the taste of the
greater public and to realise that his job is nothing but
self-sacrifice.

The Theatre as an art is inconceivable unless it is
served by self-sacrificing artists, and run on a small
non-mercantile scale by people who understand the
nature of the Theatre, and make it possible to exist on
but a limited patronage. A big artistic Theatre is

D

quite impossible from the financial point of view unless it is supported for quite a long time as an institution of culture by the Government or by private individuals.

The big Imperial Theatres in Russia were founded, apart from the idea of providing entertainment for the public, as institutions for the encouragement of art and artists, and for popular education. In Russia, from the 18th century to the present day under the Soviet régime, the Theatre, on account of its emotional and popular appeal has been considered by the government as being the most powerful medium for stimulating thought and the imagination, for encouraging a sense of beauty, and for interpreting life, and has held the same status as the national Museums, scientific Academies and Universities. Theatres in Russia are subsidised by the Government as institutions inseparable from the future development of the country. " Subsidised," however, does not imply that they are insufficiently patronised. The annual subsidy for the five Imperial Theatres (£200,000 in 1916) made it possible to experiment and to wait until the public grew accustomed to and accepted new plays, new actors, new producers and scenic artists. Quite a large proportion of the subsidy was used for purposes other than the running expenses—such as theatrical schools and the upkeep of large offices and of quite an army of unnecessary Court officials attached to the Theatres.

Here are the returns of the performances in some of

the Imperial Theatres since 1897, showing how the receipts increased with the higher standard of the productions.

Moscow Grand Theatre   (Ballet).

1897	Average return per performance :				£100
1899	,,	,,	,,	,,	£170
1901	,,	,,	,,	,,	£200
1913	,,	,,	,,	,,	£300

Petersburg Imperial Marie Theatre   (Opera).

1897	Average return per performance				£300
1913	,,	,,	,,	,,	£400

The average return per performance in the Petersburg Alexandra Dramatic Theatre in 1913 was about £130, and in the Moscow Little Dramatic Theatre—which was smaller than the Alexandra Theatre—about £120.

When one is reminded that the seats in those theatres were not expensive (the highest price for a front stall being about 8s. and the cheapest seat about 9d.), even the most sceptical " commercial " manager must agree that the business in those theatres, producing as they did, so many of the uncommercial " artistic " plays, was at least good.

The Directors of private dramatic and operatic Theatres in Russia, regarded the Theatre from more or less the same point of view as the Government, the attitude of nearly everyone who worked in our Theatres.

We need not conclude from this, however, that
Theatre Directors in Russia had no desire to earn their
living or that the actors were all ready to sacrifice
themselves and were indifferent to good salaries, but
rather that they looked for financial success only as the
result of genuine artistic work, and not from providing
people with cheap entertainment.   If, from time to
time, they descended to the latter expedient it was
merely to enable them to give other productions of
real artistic merit at a later date.   Although, as in any
other country, there were cases of theatrical bankruptcy,
they were not due to the artistry of the productions,
but were generally the direct result of mismanagement.
Naturally the theatres of the daring experimental
type ran at a loss, but frequently even these theatres,
" The Moscow Art Theatre " for example, not only
eventually paid their way but showed a good profit.   I
cannot recall any Russian theatrical Director who, like
his colleagues in the West, regarded his profession as a
gamble.   Even the Director who was very keen on the
matter of profits always had something of the artist in
him and therefore the so called " commercial " theatre
was quite unknown in Russia.

Since the Russian Director did not back a play
financially in the same spirit as one backs a horse—
i.e. on the chance of it proving a winner—as mostly
happens in London, Paris and New York—there was
no need for him to run big risks.   In the first place he
never backed a single play, but a *repertory* season, or even
a few seasons of plays which lasted from five to nine

months, when the most successful productions from the financial point of view were able to support the less successful until the latter began to pay their way. For instance in my Moscow repertory Theatre, Mozart's opera "Il Seraglio"—which began its run to a house three-quarters empty—was, by the aid of other pieces, playing three months later to capacity. The Russian Directors never lost sight of the fact that good plays are useless for purposes of speculation and long runs, and realised that they must be produced under conditions which would make it possible for them to pay, *i.e.*, in repertory Theatres. Secondly, when making his budget for the season, the Director usually allowed a maximum of 40 or 50 per cent. of the night's capacity takings for the total cost of the night's running expenses, and he would never indulge in such ridiculous fancies as to have, for instance, a capacity house of £250 per night with expenses at £200 per night, as I have seen in the Western " commercial" Theatre. Thirdly, like the astute proprietor of a magazine, he offered his patrons a variety of interesting international material, which afforded his artistes every opportunity to display their versatility. Thus the Russian Director was not merely able to draw the same public again and again to his theatre, as the magazine owner induces the same people to buy his paper every week, but he stimulated variety of output in the playwright and encouraged the real art of acting. Every dramatic and operatic Theatre in Moscow and Petersburg had a definite policy, which

resulted in the public being interested in a particular
Theatre as in an artistic institution, and not only in
certain plays and certain actors.   The run of a season
at some of these theatres was even assured beforehand
by the subscriptions for seats for all the coming plays,
as in the Theatre Guild of New York.   Again, as the
Russian Director engaged his company, not on the
chance of the successful run of a single play, but for a
whole season or even several seasons, he was able to
obtain the best actors for half the salary which they
would have demanded had they been engaged for the
run of a single piece.   Futhermore, he had the time
and opportunity to discover new talent among the
minor and younger members of his company and to
give them the chance to rise in their profession.   Also,
not to be overlooked is the fact that by affording his
artistes an assured income for a considerable period, he
influenced the box office receipts in his favour, since
he got better work out of them and greater enthusiasm
than if they had been faced from the moment of
engagement with the possibility of again being at a
loose end in a week or two, as nine times out of ten is
the case in the West End of London or in New York.

Although there are quite a number of good actors on
the commercial stage to-day, bad acting predominates,
much of which is due not only to the directly corrupt
influence of the inartistic requirements of the commercial managers and producers, but also to the
miserable economic straits which so many actors and
actressess are called upon to face.   The commercial

"THE TALES OF HOFFMAN," by Offenbach. The Prologue. Moscow, 1919. Komisarjevsky.

actor's ever present fear of being out of work is mainly responsible for " cabotinage " on the commercial stage. A " cabotin " actor, in his effort to retain his position on the stage and rise in his profession and salary, really thinks of nothing but himself and is jealous and afraid of everyone and everything. Team-work or the play mean little to him, his only desire is to exhibit *himself* to the greatest possible advantage, thereby nullifying the efforts of others. When he finds that certain aspects of his " personality " and a few stage tricks please the audience and therefore pay well, he exploits them for all he is worth over and over again until he is incapable of anything else. An actor of this sort, the product of the " commercial " theatre, is a shameless self-exhibitor, an assassin of a play and an enemy to the Theatre. Duse, referring to these people, said they poisoned even the air and expressed the wish that they might die of the plague.

Returning to the Russian Director—the Western Theatre suffers from one great handicap which he was not called upon to face, and that is the exhorbitant rents demanded in London, for instance. In Russia, even from the legal point of view—apart from its moral aspect—speculation in leases of theatres would have been considered a matter for criminal proceedings in the Courts. It would be thought incredible, for instance, that anyone could take a theatre for £75 a week, then sub-let it to someone else for £150, who, in his turn, let it to another for

£300, who once again sub-lets it at a profit to somebody else, until finally the producer of a play is permitted to use the bare walls of the theatre for the handsome weekly rental of £500 or even more—the last three or four weeks of the lease to be paid in advance at the time of signing the agreement!

In Russia before the Revolution, every provincial town had one or more theatrical building belonging to the Municipality which were let to Managers on a reasonable percentage basis. Some of these Municipalities even paid a subsidy to the Directors. If a Theatre were taken at a fixed rent in the centre of Moscow or Petersburg it amounted to a sum averaging £40 per week. These theatres were leased fully equipped direct to the Director without the profiteering " middle-man," who is so much to blame in London for the present state of the theatre.

But whatever responsibility may rest with this " incubus " for the condition of the English, French and American Theatre, there is no need to delude ourselves into imagining, as some people do, that merely lowering rents and reducing the prices of seats would induce the public to flock to the Theatre in very much greater numbers than they do to-day.

Just as the masses never overcrowd the good picture galleries, or concerts of the best music, and very seldom read good books, so they would never fill artistic Theatres to the extent which would make them a money making proposition. The artistic Theatre looks for its existence solely among those

people who love and understand art or who are
sufficiently keen to learn to understand it. The greater
public would only go to an artistic show if for some
reason the said show became fashionable or if it
offered something sufficiently topical or sensational.
Artistic Theatres without big capital behind them
could only survive nowadays if their leaders (producers) were artistes of a self-sacrificing nature with
definite ideas and with practical commonsense, who
surrounded themselves with good actors sharing their
ideas and willing to sacrifice their vanity and comfort
for the sake of the Theatre in which they worked.
Low rent and inexpensive seats are essentials, but the
spirit of the whole enterprise, the quality of its work
and the management of the Theatre would be far
more important. If the producer were not a real
master with a full knowledge of every branch of
Theatrical art and did not understand the peculiarities
of the business side of an artistic Theatre (which has
very little in common with the business of the
" commercial " Theatre) even a house given to him
rent-free could not save him from failure. An
artistic Theatre must be a repertory Theatre and must
have a definite idealistic policy in the production of
its plays, which would make the public accept that
particular Theatre. Above all, in its choice of plays,
methods of production, and acting, it should be an
experimental and advanced Theatre. It must have a
permanent company of good, enthusiastic and vital
actors, who would demonstrate the ideas of the

producer, understand and like his methods of working, be trained by him into a harmonious team and who would be willing to work on a *co-operative* basis. In such a Theatre expenses must be reduced to a minimum and fortunes cannot be spent, as in the " commercial " Theatre, on quite unnecessary " star " actors, on different useless employees, mostly indulging in a " dolce far niente," on extravagant publicity and on " beautiful spectacular productions." The producer of an artistic Theatre must know the secret of producing plays as cheaply as possible, but at the same time as perfectly and as impressively as possible. All the Theatres of our time, which make any approach to the ideal of an artistic Theatre and are not subsidised by anybody, such as, Charles Dullin's " Atelier," Louis Jouvet's, Gaston Baty's and George Pitoeff's Theatres in Paris, Delacre's Theatre in Brussels, Bragaglia's in Italy, Nigel Playfair's Theatre in London, etc., are run more or less on the lines which I am here indicating. The " Barnes " Theatre, although miles from the West End of London, succeeded in remaining open for one year and drew an ever increasing public with each new production, because of a stable policy and a sincere and original manner of acting and producing, which was established by me during my work there (from December, 1925, until the end of 1926) on " Ivanov," " Uncle Vanya," " The Three Sisters " and " The Cherry Orchard " by Chehov, " Katerina " by Andreyev, and " The Government Inspector " by Gogol. The Barnes Theatre would still be open and

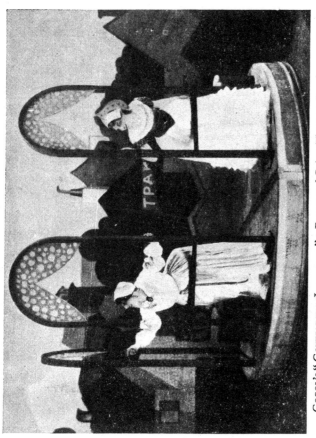

Gogol's "Government Inspector." Barnes and Gaiety Theatres, London, 1926.
Komisarjevsky.

paying its way now, as it did then, if my friend Philip Ridgeway, who was the Director, had not suddenly acquired ideas in other directions. He wanted to start " commercial " work in the heart of London and employ " stars " who draw the large public instead of those good but then unknown actors of the Barnes seasons (amongst whom were Jean Forbes Robertson, Jeanne de Casalis, Dorothy Dix, Martita Hunt, Dorothy Massingham, Hilda Sims, R. Farquharson, I. Swinley, Z. Gielgud, Dan Roe, Guy Pelham Boulton, Claude Rains, Charles Laughton and others), and wished to put on musical comedies instead of the good Russian, and other good plays by English authors, which I intended to produce later at the Barnes Theatre. I cannot altogether blame Ridgeway for giving up the management of the Barnes Theatre owing to the more than trying and unfavourable conditions under which we were obliged to work in order to keep going, and he is certainly to be congratulated on having started such a venture, which doubtlessly influenced the English stage of to-day to a very considerable extent. However, closed or open, the Barnes Theatre proved, as the Lyric, Hammersmith, is proving still, that even in London where interest in the real art of the Theatre is even smaller than in other big cities, successful artistic enterprise although very difficult is still possible. " I have never known "—writes the great English actress Mrs. Patrick Campbell in her book —" the *art* of acting really cared for in this country."

The intellectual crisis through which the world has been passing since the war is not only responsible for the extremely bad taste of the greater public everywhere, and therefore for the lack of interest in the good Theatre, but also for the dearth of good plays and good actors. Charles Dullin has said that of 1,500 manuscripts of plays sent to him in Paris in a single year, 1,400 were absolutely valueless. If someone were to ask me how many of the 1,500 actors whom I know in England were *good* actors, I should probably not even find the hundred that Dullin found among his 1,500 plays, and even then about 80 per cent of them would probably be poisoned by the mercantilism of the commercial stage, either earning tons of money or rolling about in motor-cars waiting for a good job, and looking with a condescending smile upon the down-at-heel artistic producer, in old hat, second-hand suit, and a tie which does not exactly harmonise with his shirt, and who has to look twice in his pocket before boarding a common 'bus. The work of a non-commercial producer under such conditions is somewhat similar to the man who tries to break a wall with his head. Yet, if he possesses those qualities, which, according to a famous English veteran actress, are necessary for a girl who wants to go on the modern stage, *i.e.* the hide of a rhinoceros, the courage of a lion and the endurance of an arctic explorer, there is some hope that he may not split his skull completely and be able to make at least a small aperture in that wall which stands between him and the realisation of his artistic aspirations.

The reasons why the *commercial* Theatre is not sufficiently patronized are manifold.

First of all the Theatre, because of its æsthetic and intellectual nature, is not and never was a commercial institution. The commercial managers, although they make a pretence of giving the greater public what it wants, merely guess at *everybody's* taste and of course in most cases wrongly. Then—the stale plots and the old traditional forms of " mises-en-scene " and acting which the commercial producers, frightened of experiments and risks, persist in employing *ad nauseam* not only do not appeal to the modern mentality but are no longer convincing and often merely ridiculous. The formidable over-production of theatrical shows, the very high prices of very uncomfortable seats, the competition of the Cinema, which offers the public more imaginative and up-to-date performances with good seats and for less money, are other causes of the so-called " depression " in the commercial Theatre.

While speaking of the uncommercial nature of the Theatre I must make an exception, however strange it may seem, in the case of occasional musical comedies and certain " revues." These shows at times even artistic, frequently prove good commercial propositions. There can be no doubt that gay singing, music, dancing and colour, blended with light comedy plots and appealing much more to the public's emotions than to its intellect, are strong enough to excite the

imagination of even the dullest, and to induce them
to accept the artistry.   Besides, although from the
literary and musical point of view the majority of
modern musical comedies and revues are just as far
removed from art as any other commercial show, and
the acting, singing, and dancing found in them very
often merely serve as a disguise for the true prostitu-
tional aims of these productions, the vitality, spontaneity and versatility demanded of the leading modern
exponents of these shows obliges them to use their
imaginations and perfect their technique to a much
greater degree than is demanded of the commercial
dramatic actors.

The speculation in the rents of theatres is a direct
result of the gambling spirit of commercial Theatrical
enterprise as a whole.   Why should not those who
own theatre leases profiteer when the sole ambition
of managers and producers is to pull off a successful
gamble ?

Since I have often been told by people in the
business side of the commercial Theatre, when
speaking of artistic productions and first-rate acting
that they were " too good," I am forced to the con
clusion that the gamble in the commercial Theatre is
on the bad taste of the public.   Moreover, as I have
been further informed by commercial managers and
producers that to be a success a commercial show
" must not make people think," I presume that the
commercial Theatre speculates also on the stupidity
of the public.

Apart from those good plays which by some strange chance occasionally find their way on to the commercial stage, the typical commercial productions with their endless repetitions of a couple of stale plots, the characters one has seen so often, the inevitable " laughs," the same inhuman criminal and detective jig-saw problems, the same " thrills " and " sexual attractions," the same producer's and actor's tricks, confine their appeal to the public's poorest intellects and really under-estimate the average intelligence.

If there are people who derive pleasure from listening to platitudes, or from having their minds reduced to a state of inanity, or from having their murderous or sexual instincts publicly tickled, why, one may well ask, should the institutions, which provide these forms of entertainment, be called " Theatres " ? Some of the houses catering for sexual indulgence in Paris offer little shows to their patrons called " attractions inédites " and " tableaux vivants très éxcitants," which differ but slightly from the sex-appeal stuff of the commercial stage. Why should not these places also rejoice in the name of " Theatres " ? Or why should not the commercial theatre call itself by a word more indicative of its true character ? There is no doubt that the commercial manager would not entertain the suggestion. He would not admit as frankly as the manager in Zola's " Nana," that his Theatre at the time when certain productions were running was merely a brothel. He knows only too well that the majority of the public would not go so readily to his show if its true character were not obscured by the noble name of Theatrical art, which he so much despises in his heart. I am no Puritan and a work of art is far from being a sermon, but at the same time it would be nonsense to assert that Theatrical art has nothing to do with morality. Above all, an actor cannot, like a painter or writer, separate himself from his work, and he himself is his " œuvre." An actor gives on the stage a public exhibition of his body, and if he cannot make the spectator feel that body to be merely a vehicle for the purposes of expressing the working of his mind, his performance is not far removed from prostitution. Everything an actor does on the stage is dependent on the idealistic motive behind that action. From the moral point of view it is not *what* he does that matters but rather *how* he does it. A prudish situation or gesture can be made immoral by the thought of the actor at the moment (we have many examples of it in commercial hypocritically " clean " shows) and on the other hand the most realistically " shocking " one can be mastered by a real artist of the stage into a work of art because of the spiritual significance he gives it.

That I may conclude this chapter and as far as possible not return to the commercial Theatre, let us follow a modern theatrical gambler or so-called " manager " into his office and see him at work. As an example let me take one whom I knew in one of the countries of the commercial Theatre.

That gentleman, as often happens, had no Theatre and no company of his own, had never witten a play, and knew not a thing about producing one, had never acted or been even an " A.S.M.," but he had very smart offices in the heart of the city, a pretty secretary, and was on the look out for plays. Whenever he discovered what he thought to be a good financial proposition, he would try to find someone with money—for the very good reason that he lacked that essential commodity himself—who might be justly termed a sort of " milch-cow," but in the profession called a " backer." Having found the backer, he would induce him to put up the necessary cash with which to launch his money-making play.

In face of the number of failures in Paris, the West End of London and New York—(there was a time during the winter of 1928–29, when about forty Houses were closed in the latter, and in the West End of London during a period of about five months of the same season, not mentioning the semi-commercial failures and all the " musical " flops, sixteen truly commercial dramatic plays completely failed, having each an average run of only fourteen performances, and those patronized mostly by " complimentary " spectators, which resulted in a loss of about £100,000) —it seems incredible that such backers should still be forthcoming, but apparently the supply is not yet quite exhausted. This is so because the manager has the boldness to assure the backer that the play is a " certain winner " and that the " stars " he

E

has engaged are very big draws, and holds out the prospect of a fantastic return for his money, such as would be unheard of in any normally regulated business. He tells him, for instance, of a lucky author of a musical comedy who has lately made £30,000 out of the run of one of his pieces, or of a bank clerk who made as much as he could have earned in twenty years as a bank clerk out of a play running during the London Season. But he obviously forgets to remind him that the very stars he has engaged have previously been in failure after failure of certain winners and have lost their backers hundreds of thousands of pounds. If the backer—usually a business man—is not greatly impressed by the actual business ability of the manager (how could he be ?), he will sometimes allow his sporting spirit to get the better of him, and the prospect of personal " kudos " may further influence his better judgment. He regards the whole affair as he would gambling at Monte Carlo or backing a horse—he takes a chance . . . and usually loses.

I was once intimately acquainted with one of these backers. He kept a shoe shop and went to every first night. But he could never make up his mind if the show were good or bad until in the intervals he heard the opinion of other people. He loved the Theatre, but still more the society of female members of the theatrical profession, and to be able to say that he knew " So and So " and was quite at home behind the scenes of half a dozen theatres. Within my own knowledge he backed seven plays and lost on all of them. As he was very good-natured and possessed plenty of money, he never grumbled and took the failures as bad luck, and was dubbed " a real sport " by the manager whom he had lavishly supplied with cash.

How certain the managers themselves actually are of their " certain winners " was made manifest to me by the state of panic in which a certain manager with whom I was acquainted usually found himself during the period of rehearsal and particularly after the dress rehearsal. He insisted breathlessly on cuts and alterations on the ground that the public wouldn't like this or that, and frantically mutilated plays until they became almost unrecognisable. The mutilation of plays is, by the way, one of the features of commercial productions. I remember two plays I produced in the West End of London which were completely distorted by the aid of managerial improvements. One of them was originally a very good fantastic ensemble play, but it was obvious to me from reading it that it was not the sort of thing to draw the West End public. To make a commercial proposition out of it, the managers turned it into a star show and by so doing upset its acting balance. By trying to adapt the play to the " realistic taste of the London public," they altered the whole meaning of it and reduced it to complete absurdity. The play, which would have been an artistic success in any normal Theatre, was a complete failure because of all this commercial treatment. The other play was a pleasant French "pièce de théâtre," but he who adapted it " to suit English taste " deprived it of all vitality and made the characters inconsistent. When I told my management what I thought of the adaptation they replied something to the effect that it was what the public wants. During rehearsals the star-actors began, in their turn, to alter the play, re-writing it, transposing scenes, etc. As they were engaged, as is mostly the case, merely because of their box-office drawing power and not for the reason that they suited the parts, they tried to adapt the play so that they might be able to exhibit their personalities and their stock tricks to the best advantage. Up to the last moment I had the naïve hope of being able to persuade everyone to return to the original script of the play, but in this I failed and after a few performances the " certain winner " disappeared for ever with my fee (of which I never got a penny) and a couple of thousand of the poor backers' banknotes.

I cannot call the incompetent game of chance played by the commercial Theatre a legitimate business, and the term " commercial " in such a connection seems to be very ironical.

The commercial Theatre resembles a huge factory, backed by eccentric capitalists, which goes on producing a poor assortment of cheap stuff for the masses which no one really wants. The factory goes smash at frequent intervals, but strange as it may seem a new capitalist and his money is always forthcoming to

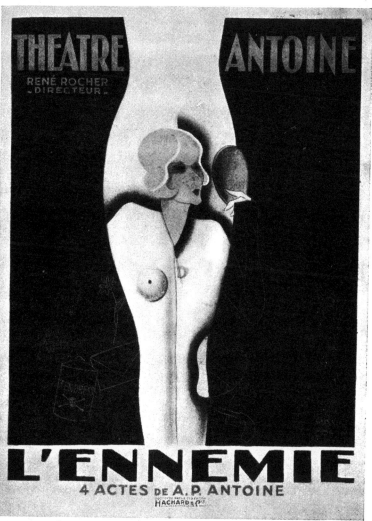

FRENCH POSTER OF A COMMERCIAL PLAY, which was written by Antoine, but not by the great artistic producer of the same name, and produced at the Theatre Antoine, named so " in honour " of the great producer.

save it at the critical moment. Occasionally some pleasing ingredient is offered as a bait for the goods and the masses rush to buy them. The last capitalist, ignoring the losses which hundreds of previous capitalists have suffered before him in financing the factory, draws all the profits himself. Then the time comes when the masses again tire of the stuff and the demand for it ceases, and the last capitalist withdraws all his money, making room for the next quixotic business man, and the game begins all over again. . . .

CHAPTER THREE

THE first rehearsal I ever held was a great lesson to
me and ever since I have understood the value of
patience and presence of mind for a producer.
Although always keen on trying to do new things and
never really afraid of the unpleasantness and hostility
arising from experimenting, the reception I received
from the company at that rehearsal made me feel not a
little apprehensive.

When I entered the auditorium the actors, with
all of whom I was on friendly terms, responded very
stiffly to my greetings. I made an effort, however,
to appear unconcerned and started the rehearsal; but
the actors, though doing everything they were told,
made not the slightest effort to "act."

Apart from the fact that as experienced actors they
could not possibly submit without protest to the
directions of an inexperienced young man who had
never produced anything in his life, and, who was

moreover, one of those who had " a lot of foolish, new-fangled notions " in his head, there were also other reasons for their attitude. Some who were friends of Meyerhold, the producer, were hostile because he had preceded me in the rehearsal of this very play but had had to leave the Theatre on account of differences with the management. Again, others who had disliked Meyerhold and his methods (strangely enough, the majority of actors dislike anything new in the Theatre) were afraid that I might work on similar lines.

After keeping my patience with great effort for an hour, I could stand it no longer, and blowing out the candle on the producer's desk, said something rude and left the Theatre without hat and coat. Later on I was very ashamed of this exhibition of youthful temper. Probably the fact that I had fallen in love at the time with a certain girl, while another was pursuing me, added to my nervousness. The night before this rehearsal I was leaving the house of the girl with whom I was in love (she had a lovely round face, eyes like a young calf and very fair hair) when the other girl, who was spying upon me, stopped me in the street and made a terrific scene ; she swore she would throw herself into the Neva and actually flung fifty roubles that she had borrowed from me a month before into the snow. To pacify her I had to take her home and remain talking to her (to the great indignation of her landlady) until three o'clock in the morning. The next day, before the rehearsal, I rang up the round faced girl, who, to my horror, told me that she had seen me through the window leaving her house with another woman, and calling me various pleasant names added that I had ruined her life for ever and that she was through with me and now intended to kill herself.   As it was the first time in my life that such a complication had occurred, I felt like a criminal and was the most wretched man on earth, particularly so since neither girl would let me see her again, and I was in hourly expectation of hearing that something terrible had happened to both of them.   However, nothing did happen, and in about a year's time they were both happily married.

The first night of this play—which I produced after all, as the company later adopted a friendly attitude towards me—was not less tragi-comic than its first rehearsal.   The play was an unusual one, a kind of a miracle with the action happening simultaneously on two floors into which the stage was divided.   On the " ground floor " was Hell with a crowd of tailed, up-to-date devils reading newspapers and making topical remarks.   Above was the Earth, showing a monastery courtyard.   (The setting was designed by M. Doboujinsky.)   At the end of the play a certain Saint who lived in the monastery was saved by Divine intervention from being swallowed by an enormous dragon sent from Hell.   The play was called " The Devil's Show " and was written by one of the best modern Russian poets, Alexis Remizov. (Remizov looks like a dear little devil and lives at

VERA KOMISARJEVSKY IN "THE TWO FATES"

the present moment in exile in Paris, as do many other important Russian writers, such as D. Merejkovsky, Ivan Bounin, Kouprin, etc.) During the performance the audience was restless but quiet. With the fall of the curtain, however, there was a mixed reception of boos, whistles and cheers. In spite of this we took no less than twenty calls, and the effect of the play was such that people actually fought in the auditorium because of the difference in opinion.

All this happened in St. Petersburg in 1907 in Vera Komisarjevsky's (my sister's) Theatre. This was a troubled time for the Theatre in those places where the art of the Theatre mattered—it was in fact a period of a new Theatrical revolution. This revolution was directed against the realistic acting and the realistic *mises-en-scène* first employed by André Antoine in 1886 at the " Theatre Libre " in Paris.

Antoine, who began his life as a poor employee in a Gas Company and is now a famous critic in Paris, challenged the routine of the French Theatres with his realistic productions, which aimed at expressing " the spiritual truth of life in forms of actuality." He found inspiration in the works of writers—realists like Zola, the Goncourts, Henri Becque, Courteline, L. Tolstoy, G. Hauptmann, etc., and in the acting of various great individual performers—realists. Although Antoine advanced much further he was influenced by the " naturalistic " productions of the German Meininger Company, which was founded by the Duke George II

of Saxen-Meiningen in 1874. The Meininger wanted
to bring the stage closer to life and fought the existing
stage routine and deteriorated traditions of the
romantic school of acting. The " sublime, exalted,
and heroic " manner of the acting of Talma, Mlle.
Mars, Mlle. George, the Keans, Phelps and other
romantics had had an enormous influence and left
many imitators. Even to-day the European stage is
not free from the stale traditions of the romantics,
the modern English " Shakespearean " acting being
one of the many examples of this tradition. At the
beginning of our century Mounet Sully of the Comédie
Française was still acting in the romantic and even
the classic manner, and Beerbohm Tree in England
succeeded in combining his " star " methods of acting
and the " Shakespearean " tradition with some of the
" Meininger " tricks. One of the aims of the
Meininger, however, was to abolish that " star "
system, which had originated in the classic Theatre
of the seventeenth and eighteenth centuries and which
because of its appropriateness to the individual
philosophy of romanticism had been adopted by the
romantic Theatre. In the productions of the Duke
George, the actors instead of playing for themselves,
as was customary under the " star " system, became
dependent one upon the other, thus creating an
" ensemble." They did not rant, pose, or give
exhibitions of simulated temperament so characteristic
of the traditional romantic acting, but had to behave
" naturally " on the stage, representing life-like types

without any conscious playing to the audience.   They
had to look to actual life for characteristic intonations,
faces, gestures, attitudes, and to make use of them in
their parts with the assistance of assumed voices,
complicated make-ups, padding, etc.   Acting in this
way, the bad actors of the Meininger troupe looked
very much as if animated figures were moving about
in Madame Tussaud's " natural " surroundings.

Kronegg, the producer of the Meininger, introduced
the method of teaching actors like parrots.   He gave
them every inflection and gesture and moved them
about at rehearsals on a floor marked out with chalk
into squares and numbers, like so many chess men.
The crowd, the small parts and the settings, as well
as naturalistic effects (thunderstorms, rain, noises of
battles, cracking floors, etc.) became for the first
time on the stage in the Meininger productions just
as important as the leading actors.

" Je reviens précisément de Bruxelles," wrote
Antoine, " où j'avais passé une quinzaine à suivre
cette troupe allemande.   Vous savez que je vais
donner cet hiver *La Patrie en Danger*, et je rêvais à ce
propos une expérience intéressante sur les foules.
Aller voir les Meininger était donc tout indiqué.

" Je suis, depuis que je vais au théâtre, embêté de
ce que nous faisons avec nos figurants.   Si j'en
excepte en effet la Haine et le cirque de Théodora,
je n'ai jamais rien vu qui m'ait donné la sensation de
la multitude.

" Eh ! bien, je l'ai vue chez les Meininger !   Leur

figuration n'est pas comme la nôtre composée d'éléments ramassés au hasard, d'ouvriers embauchés pour les répétitions générales, mal habillés et peu exercés à porter des costumes bizarres ou gênants, surtout lorsqu'ils sont exacts. L'immobilité est recommandée presque toujours au personnel de nos théâtres, tandis que là-bas, les comparses des Meininger doivent jouer et mimer leur personnage. N'entendez pas par là qu'ils forcent la note et que l'attention est détournée des protagonistes ; non, le tableau reste complet et, de quelque côté que se porte le regard, il s'accroche toujours à un détail dans la situation ou le caractère. C'est d'une puissance incomparable à certains instants.

" La troupe des Meininger compte environ soixante-dix artistes des deux sexes. Tous ceux qui ne jouent pas un rôle sont tenus de figurer dans la pièce et ceci tous les soirs. S'il y a vingt comédiens occupés, les cinquante autres, sans aucune exception même pour les chefs d'emploi, paraissent en scène aux tableaux d'ensemble et chacun est le chef, le caporal d'un groupe de figurants proprement dits, qu'il dirige et qu'il surveille tant que l'on est sous l'œil du public. Cette obligation est telle que la femme de Hans de Bulow, l'une des étoiles des Meininger, ayant refusé ce service, qu'elle trouvait au-dessous de son talent, fut congédiée, bien que son mari eût le titre et les fonctions de maître de chapelle du duc de Saxe. Il quitta lui aussi, la cour ducale à la suite des incidents que provoqua ce conflit.

" Ils obtiennent ainsi des groupements d'une vérité

extraordinaire. Mais allez donc appliquer ceci sur nos théâtres et exiger même d'un comédien de cinquième ordre qu'il meuble le salon de la princesse de Bouillon ! Eh ! bien, les Meininger s'y plient ! Mlle. Lindner, leur étoile, jouant la scène du Temps dans Un Conte d'Hiver, figurait au tableau du lit de justice et mimait une femme du peuple avec autant de conscience et de soin qu'elle en apportait le lendemain soir à interpréter le rôle capital d'Hermione dans la même pièce.

" Voilà le secret de leurs foules qui sont absolument supérieures aux nôtres. Et je crois bien que, si vous aviez vu l'arrestation de Guillaume Tell et la scène de la pomme, vous auriez été ravi comme moi.

" Il y avait dans ce Guillaume Tell une autre chose superbe : le meurtre de Gessler, arrêté sur un praticable étroit, formant chemin creux, à huit mètres au moins de la rampe, par une mendiante et ses deux enfants qui jouaient de dos une longue scène de supplication, barrant la route de leur corps, pendant que Tell visait Gessler. Vous auriez convenu là qu'un dos montré à propos donne bien au public la sensation qu'on ne s'occupe pas de lui et que c'est arrivé.

" Pourquoi ces choses neuves, logiques et pas du tout coûteuses ne viendraient-elles pas remplacer ces insupportables conventions que tout le monde subit chez nous sans savoir pourquoi ?

" La seule et sincère objection que je trouve à leur faire est celle-ci : c'est que dans ce même Guillaume Tell, par exemple, Schiller ayant écrit un rôle pour la foule, tous les figurants criaient la même phrase et en mesure. C'est lourd et faux. Mais ne pourrait-on résoudre les répliques de cette foule en une rumeur savamment combinée ?

" Si nous lui faisons crier : ' Vive Gambetta ! ' par exemple, savez-vous ce que je ferais ?

" Je diviserais mes deux cents comparses en une dizaine de groupes, si vous voulez : des femmes, des enfants, des bourgeois, etc. Je ferais partir ces bourgeois *Vi* . . . , les femmes accélérant le rythme, commenceraient lorsque les autres attaquent *gam*, et je ferais traîner les gamins cinq secondes après tout le monde. C'est, en somme, un chœur à régler. Je suis bien sûr que la salle entendrait, dans une grande rumeur, Vive Gambetta ! et si, comme le font les Meininger, les attitudes, les gestes, les groupements étaient diversifiés et variés avec le même soin, nul doute que l'effet général et vrai ne se produisît.

" Dans les tableaux d'ensemble, le protagoniste tenant la scène peut rendre les silences vrais par un geste, un cri, un mouvement. Et si la foule écoute et voit l'acteur, au lieu de regarder dans la salle, ou, comme à la Comédie-Francaise, de contempler les sociétaires avec une muette, mais visible déférence, on trouvera naturel qu'elle écoute et que deux cents personnes se taisent ensemble, dominées, pour entendre un personnage qui intéresse chacun."

The old conventional décors—cut cloth " arches " with buildings, halls, gardens or forests painted on them in perspective ; " borders " of clouds, ceilings, of painted leaves, stuck on nets ; picture backings and " Molièresque " interiors, made of three flats with as many doors and windows in them as the action required—all these conventionalities were banished from the Meininger stage.   They introduced the idea of the fourth wall, the half-circular sky-cloth (cyclorama) and sets which had to be faithful copies of nature, or of rooms in which real people could live.

But infatuated with the idea of being as natural as possible, and of giving the audience the illusion that they were watching, as through a key-hole some intimate events in actual life, the Meininger overlooked the fact that the real function of the theatre is not to copy life, but to interpret plays, in which life and characters are recreated by the imagination of the dramatist, and to find for each of them a suitable form of artistic expression on the stage.   The Meininger were merely adapting plays to their aims of reproducing " natural " people in such surroundings that were photographically true to life or to historical documents.

Antoine, in his productions, did not copy actual life photographically, but looked for such life-like forms as would be expressive for the purpose of interpreting the *realistic* plays he was producing, and create the right atmosphere in such plays.

In 1890, after the failure at the Comédie Française of " La Parisienne," written by Henri Becque, Antoine wrote the following letter to the omnipotent critic Sarcey, who did his best to ridicule Becque's realistic efforts in the Press :—" The new (or renewed) Theatre needs new (or renewed) interpreters.   In order to get into the skin of modern characters all the old paraphernalia must be laid aside.   A realistic play must be *acted.* . . . The characters of " La Parisienne " are *people like ourselves.*   They don't live in large stagey halls the size of cathedrals ; they live in interiors like our own, they sit by the fireside, beneath a lamp, or round a table, and not in the least as in the old repertoire—before the footlights.   They have voices like *ours,* their language is *our* language and not that of the rhetorical high-flown style of the old plays. When the actress who played the leading part in " La Parisienne " last night spoke as an *actress,* and her partner answered her like one of Moliere's lovers, they were not true to Becque's conception, and they played false for three hours !   The important thing in the new Theatre is the total absence of self-consciousness on the part of the characters as in real life where people are not for ever conscious of what they are saying or doing.   Last night we merely saw so many actors strutting and reciting, instead of the people created by Becque. . . . Did you ever in your life see Parisian middle-class people living in such a drawing-room, without a single corner, a place where people are supposed to be able to talk and be comfortably lazy after the day's work ?   I know your objection : the scenery is of secondary importance. Yes, possibly !   But why not have it truly characteristic ?   Shouldn't scenery play as important a role

in the theatre as description does in a novel ?   Does
not the scenery serve as an environment for the story
of the play ?   It is, of course, impossible to be absolutely true to nature in the Theatre, because there are
certain conventions on the stage, but why not try to
reduce those conventions to a minimum ?   What
would become of a realistic play, full of life and
intimacy, in a falsified atmosphere ? . . . Last night
the movements were understood as badly as the
environment.   They were arranged, not according
to the text of the play and the meaning of the scenes,
but according to the whims and caprices of the actors,
each of whom played for himself alone without giving
a thought to the others.   As a matter of fact, they
were all hypnotised by the footlights !   Everyone
did his utmost to be as near as possible to the audience.
I have heard of cases in the time of gas lighting in
which actors actually burned their trousers through
hugging the footlights !   Not once did the players
look at each other while speaking.   In real life you
would say :—Look at me, damn you !   It is to you
that I am speaking !—to anyone whom you were
addressing who behaved as they did.   The truth is
that the new theatre needs new interpreters."

In the same letter he says that once when rehearsing
a play he could not make an actor even move across
the stage towards a table and sit in an armchair without
glancing at the auditorium or striking a special attitude.
" I must admit," says he, " that the actor knew his
job, but he had lost simplicity and was incapable of

F

acting as if no one were looking at him. . . . For actors who are tied to the old tradition, the stage is a sort of tribune and not an enclosed spot where something happens."

It does not seem possible that thirty-nine years have passed since this letter was written, seeing that those things of which Antoine complained are still to be seen in most of the commercial and even " realistic " artistic shows of to-day.

Still the principles of the realistic acting and the realistic *mises en scene* expounded by Antoine combined with the naturalism of the Meininger found followers and imitators throughout the theatrical world. In Germany Otto Brahm and others began producing in the realistic manner; in 1898 Stanislavsky and Vladimir Nemirovich-Danchenko opened the Moscow Art Theatre and there continued to bring the art of the Theatre closer to life, employing in their first productions the Antoine and the Meininger methods, which resulted, while working on " The Sea Gull " of Chehov, in the discovery of the impressionistic method of acting. " The most important thing in my production of *The Fruits of Enlightment* "—wrote Stanislavsky, speaking about the pre-Chehovian period of his work—" seemed to me at the time to be the contrast between the sets for the kitchen and those for the drawing room. I began to seek truth in the immediate environment of the actor and that made me realise that there must necessarily be something very akin to real life in acting too." In England

"WALKURE." The first act. 1923. Komisarjevsky.

artists in the Theatre, like Robertson, the Bancrofts, and Granville Barker, who is one of the inspired and subtle producers of our time, but who has unfortunately for the English Stage, almost deserted it, were representative of the realistic school, and in America the apostle of the realistic *mises en scene* was David Belasco. Of course realism in England could never be and was not the intense Continental " naked truth of life." To suit the public's taste, life on the English stage had to be shown through a mist of loveliness. On the modern commercial stage the methods of realistic acting have degenerated into a stock of spiritless conventions as to how to pretend to be natural, flavoured with a little of the artificiality of the old romantic school.

Vera Komisarjevsky, unlike Antoine, was not a realist, and required other forms than those of mere actuality in order to express the spiritual truth of life in her acting. As an actress she was very economical and synthetic in her mode of expression and avoided outward typical details. She insisted that an actor's means of expression should be restricted to the simplest fundamentals in order to show the essential inner life of a character. The Theatre, according to her, should find its own " theatrical " forms, independent of everyday life, to express the characters " invented " by the playwright and his ideas. While seeking these forms, she started a new theatrical movement in her Theatre which, for lack of a better name, must be called the " symbolical." The work in my sister's Theatre found its chief source of inspiration in the theories of certain Russian writers on the anti-realistic Theatre and in the ideas of Maeterlinck and of Swiss, English and German producers and scenic designers of the beginning of the twentieth century—Adolph Appia, Gordon Craig and Georg Fuchs, all of whom were the initiators of the anti-realistic theatrical revolution.

Maeterlinck, speaking about the symbolic Theatre, pointed out that its task was to produce " an *inner* drama, which has its own logic and its own development, which never coincide with the logic and the development of the events in the material outer world." According to him the symbolic Theatre has to show " the life of the soul in itself in the infinity of the universe."

Vera Komisarjevsky, who was considered " the greatest Russian actress of the beginning of the twentieth century," began her theatrical career in the nineties as an amateur in the same Moscow " Society of Art and Literature " in which Stanislavsky started, and of which my father was one of the founders. Although some of her biographers have said that she went on the stage to get away from life, this was not the case. She took up stage work because it had attracted her since childhood, because she wanted to earn her living and to be independent, and because, after her first professional season, she realized that she could act, and was encouraged to continue theatrical work. Life, without doubt, was

very unkind to her.   When a very young girl she
married a handsome painter, a Count and student of
the Imperial Academy of Arts.   She loved and trusted
him with her usual enthusiasm and abandonment.
She did not think of the stage at that time, but
arranged her life to suit him and to help him in his
work.   As they were very poor—she never wanted
to accept financial help from our father—she had to
do all the household work and denied herself everything in order to get the best for her husband.   The
first doubt crept into her mind when once, on his
return from work, she kissed him and he smelt of
oranges.   " How could he," she thought, " buy an
orange and eat it without leaving some for her when
she denied herself everything ? "   Later, when they
were staying one summer on her uncle's estate, she
returned from a day in town to find another woman,
a very near relation of hers, who was also staying in
the manor, in the arms of her husband.   This was such
a shock to Vera that she ran away and lived alone
for a time earning money by doing sewing and secre-
tarial work, until my father persuaded her to come
to him and act as his secretary.   It was at that time
that he taught her to sing (she had a very good
contralto voice) and made her take parts in the operatic
performances of his students and join the " Society
of Arts and Literature."   A well-known old actor,
Kisselevsky, who later greatly encouraged my sister
and was mainly responsible for her becoming an
actress, saw her acting for that Society, and recom-

mended her to the manager of the Novocherkask
repertory Theatre, in which Kisselevsky acted, and
persuaded her to join it. From Novocherkask she
was engaged by the repertory Theatre in Vilna, from
which in 1898 she went to the Petersburg Imperial
Theatre. Playing both dramatic and comedy parts,
with great simplicity and sincerity, " she always
seemed, by some inexplicable magic, to be much more
than merely the person she was representing." In all
the best parts in her repertoire—"Hilda" and "Nora"
in Ibsen plays, " Sonya " and " Nina " in Chehov,
" Christine " in Schnitzler, " Magda," " Rosie,"
" Marikka," " Klerchen " in Sudermann, " Beatrice "
in Maeterlinck, " Fantine " in V. Hugo, " Larissa "
in Ostrovsky, " Gretchen " in Faust, " Ophelia " in
Hamlet, etc.—she was what Goethe called " Das Ewig
Weibliche," symbolising the deepest feelings and
longings of girlhood and womanhood. " Her wide-
open blue eyes looked at us questioningly from the
stage, while her inimitable deep musical voice seemed
to be making an appeal to something beyond the
bourn of this material world as if promising to tell
a wonderful secret which everyone of us longed to
know." (Znosko Borovsky's " History of the Russian
Theatre.")

For an actress of that quality the Imperial stage of
her time, with its matter-of-fact realistic methods, was
far from the right place. Besides, my sister being of
a lively, restless nature, never really satisfied with
herself, always longing to advance in her work, was

stifled by the atmosphere of the Alexandra Theatre, which was one of accomplished, self-satisfied actors, all past masters at intrigue, of which she was quite incapable. Because of the intrigues she was not treated particularly well in that Theatre, and was not given a single new part during her last season there despite her extraordinary success with the public.

In 1902 Vera left the Imperial Theatre to tour the provinces. She wanted to make enough money to start a theatre of her own, in which she intended to put into practice her ideas on acting and the staging of plays. It was her opinion that realistic production, with a conglomeration of detail in the acting as well as in the environment of the actors, distracted the attention of the public " from the soul of the actor." She wanted " *suggestions* of things and not the things themselves." For instance, speaking of the balcony scene in " Romeo and Juliet " she said to me : " There must only be some idea of the balcony and nothing else." But she did not know how to realize what she wanted ; she was not a producer, and said that " an actor cannot produce a play if he is acting in it." In this she was right, because the point of view of a producer, who is outside the team, and that of the actor, who is in the team, is absolutely different.

After her tour, which was not only successful but triumphant, she opened her repertory " Dramatic Theatre " in Petersburg in 1904 and tried various producing directors. She was dissatisfied with all of them until in 1906 she met and engaged Vsevolod

Meyerhold, who is now the leading producer in Soviet Russia, a communist, an "Artist of the People," etc., etc. At that time he ran a provincial co-operative company "Of the New Drama," and previous to that had been an actor in the Moscow Art Theatre and assistant to Stanislavsky. When the latter under the influence of playwrights-symbolists decided to experiment in producing "new" plays, Meyerhold among other young producers, was engaged by Stanislavsky to assist him. Stanislavsky realised that the plays written by the symbolists required new methods of expression, very different from those employed by him in realistic plays ; but, as he says in his book, he "only strained toward the new methods without knowing any of the ways for reaching and realising" them. After some talks with Meyerhold, who "thought that he had already found the new ways and methods" Stanislavsky decided in 1902 to open the First Studio of the Moscow Art Theatre for experimental purposes. It seemed to Stanislavsky then that Meyerhold and himself were "seeking for one and the same thing," and that, judging from their talks and from Meyerhold's letters, the latter "would be able to introduce *impressionism* (?) in the Theatre and find a beautiful and conventionalized form for its expression." It soon became obvious, however, that Meyerhold and Stanislavsky were by no means striving after the same thing. The former attempted to put into practice his theories on stylised acting (derived from Maeterlinck) and to use the ideas of modern scenic artists of the " left " group, whom he engaged to design the sets for the Studio. Meyerhold tried to confine the actors in his productions to primitive picturesque movements and artificial intonations, making the acting subsidiary to the settings, and merely fitting the actors into the static picturesque décor. The insincere acting of the company under these conditions did not meet with Stanislavsky's approval and led to his separation from Meyerhold and to the closing of the Studio before the experimental productions could be shewn to the public. Later on Stanislavsky himself attempted to produce some symbolical plays with the Moscow Art Theatre, but these productions were not successful because Stanislavsky's realistic tendencies in direction of acting and in the details of the surroundings were never in keeping with the symbolic idea of the production as a whole. For instance, " Hamlet " on the stage of the Moscow Art Theatre became a kind of realistic " middle class " drama, performed in symbolic settings devised by Gordon Craig which demanded a similar symbolic manner of acting.

A real artist, Stanislavsky was always interested in anything new concerning the theatre, and his interest was not confined to theorising. He always experimented with new methods and principles concerning the art of acting and of production. His mentality, however, is that of a realist and his most vital quality both as actor and producer is sincerity. It is this quality, which he believes to be the most important in the performance of any actor, which has prevented him from using any other methods of expression than those of realism.   The greatness of Stanislavsky lies in his artistry in the selection of realistic forms for the sincere expression of the characters he portrays. All the parts in which Stanislavsky must be called great (Lövborg in " Hedda Gabler," Doctor Astrov in " Uncle Vanya," Doctor Stockman, etc.) and all his best productions, were created in that way.   The Moscow Art Theatre was never an exceptionally " revolutionary " institution, but it was without doubt an intellectual force, and its production of plays by Gorky, Ibsen, Hauptmann, Naidyenov, Andreyev, Chirikov, Chehov, etc., fostered the progress of the art of the Theatre and even hastened the advent of the Intellectual Revolution, which preceded the Communistic Revolution.   Since the Communistic Revolution, Stanislavsky revives plays of his old repertoire, not because he is a " reactionary," as some people think, or because he prefers them, but simply because there are no good modern Russian plays written in the realistic manner suitable for his methods, and at the same time for the present mentality of the Russian people.   He confesses in his book that " each generation has its own limitations " and that he has no desire to " rival his grandchildren." On the last European and American tour Stanislavsky was forced to do plays which he produced over twenty-five years ago, although he himself calls them

STANISLAVSKY

" old stock," and with which I believe the company was fed-up long ago.   Since he and the company required money both for their Theatre and their private needs (the great producer, I believe, had a son ill with consumption and needed money to send him to a Sanatorium) Stanislavsky had to comply with the requirements of the commercial touring managers who demanded the *famous* productions.

In my sister's Theatre Meyerhold at first succeeded, under her influence, in achieving some very convincing symbolical productions with plays such as Maeterlinck's " Sister Beatrice " with a setting by S. Soudeikine, Alexander Blok's " Show-Booth," Andreyev's " Life of Man," and Ibsen's " Hedda Gabler " with a setting by Nicolas Sapounov, a very interesting and powerful painter, a great friend of mine, who unfortunately died quite young drowned in the Gulf of Finland.   Having been for years a pupil of such a master as Stanislavsky, Meyerhold was a very good realistic producer and managed the actors and the crowds on the stage very efficiently.   But he possessed no real ideas of his own about " new " productions.   He was merely very adept at putting other people's theories into practice, and as he was a temperamental man and a good talker he was able to rouse enthusiasm in his collaborators and even make them supply him generously with their ideas.

At the time of Meyerhold's engagement at the " Dramatic Theatre," when still an undergraduate, I was asked by my sister to superintend the artistic side of her Theatre. I had to supervise the making of the scenery and to design some of the costumes, props, etc. The sketches for the dresses for " Sister Beatrice," " The Show-Booth " and " The Life of Man," together with settings for the latter play were my first work for the Theatre.

For the production of " Sister Beatrice " the only scenery Meyerhold used was a black cloth, painted in the manner of a Flemish primitive tapestry, and some steps leading off into the wings. The floor space between the decor and the footlights was very narrow and the actors were grouped like the figures in a primitive painting. The acting, stylised as regards the intonations, gestures and movement, harmonised extraordinary well with the play, as did the formal background and the music, which was by A. Liadov. The emotional effect on the public, I remember, was overwhelming, and the show was the biggest success of the St. Petersburg season. Seventy-five per cent. of that success was without doubt due to my sister's acting, but Meyerhold's production was a great step towards freeing the actor from the tyranny of life-like surroundings by doing away with them, and raising the artistic qualities of the background.

In " The Life of Man "* the characters emerged from darkness into light on to the particular spot on

* Eight months later this play was produced at the Moscow Art Theatre on the same lines as those on which we had done it, more lavishly, of course, but with setting and lighting very similar to ours.

the stage where they were to act. When the tabs parted—we had two front curtains, one drop painted by Leon Bakst, and plain blue tabs behind it—the actor who was to speak the Prologue was alone visible. As the last words of the Prologue were spoken the lights were slowly extinguished and then went up again on another part of the stage, discovering a settee with the " Old Women " on it. At the end of that scene the lights went out and a lamp on the table was switched on at the opposite side of the stage, discovering " The Relations " of " The Man " sitting round that table. The ballroom was represented by six plain heavy columns placed in a semi-circle. The scene was lighted by a specially made chandelier, which hung in the centre and threw light only on the space between the columns, so that the tops of them and the space behind them faded into darkness. Near each column was a large gilt armchair in which was seated a grotesque " Guest " of " The Man." For financial reasons we had to produce this play very quickly—in ten days—and the work on it was a " communal " effort of Meyerhold, his two assistants and myself. I remember working on the stage every night after the performances of other plays in an effort to discover how to put into practice the idea of doing away with the sets altogether, using only the necessary furniture and props. As at that time we had no special appliances to spot the stage, not enough money for black velvet to get the effect of darkness, I had to make " spots " myself of ordinary bulbs, cardboard or tin, and cover up the walls of the stage, as well as the floor, with canvas painted black. Although my sister did not act in " The Life of Man," it was another very successful production with which she was as well satisfied as she was with the other three productions which I have already mentioned. But in his subsequent productions, Meyerhold started to free himself from my sister's influence and inclined more and more towards the manner of working he had employed in Stanislavsky's Studio, confining the actors and making them dependent upon the settings instead of making the setting depend on the actor, as was the aim of my sister. In my sister's Theatre Meyerhold came to the conclusion that the unrealistic, stylised decors could not possibly harmonise with a real actor and that in order to " fit " the performer into the surroundings and to get the complete illusion of unreality on the stage, the actor must be replaced in productions where a painted back cloth is used, by a flat painted puppet, and in productions in which three-dimensional sets are used by a three-dimensional puppet. Moreover, following the idea which Gordon Craig had at one time, Meyerhold thought that a marionette, having no will of its own, would be much better material to express the producer's intentions than an actor. But instead of opening a marionette Theatre of his own, he started, for some strange reason, to fit the real actors of my sister's Theatre into an unrealistic décor, and dressed them so that they appeared to be painted or moulded on the décor.   He

"The Forest," by Ostrovsky. Moscow. Meyerhold's Theatre.

made them move like marionettes and speak—to use his own expression—as though " their words sounded like drops of water falling into a well."

After the production of " Pelleas and Melisande," Meyerhold's experiments in my sister's Theatre came to an end.   She had to part with him, realising how he cramped and limited the actors with his methods, and how his ideas at that time were leading the Theatre of living actors to a certain end.

Meyerhold was always fond of theorising and inventing new terms by which to call his methods and productions.   He talked about the " mystico-anarchic " Theatre (after a philosopher G. Chulkov), about " collectivism," when the spectators take part in a show (after Romain Rolland and V. Ivanov), " stylisation " (George Fuchs), " statuesqueness," " formalism," " conditionalism," etc.   All these terms seemed very impressive to me at the time, but failed—and fail to-day—to enable anyone to understand the idea behind his methods of production.   As far as I know, he had not the ideas about " liberating the actor," or about " antidecoration " we are told he had in Huntley Carter's book on the Theatre in Soviet Russia.   The idea that every author ought to be produced in his own style never occurred to him either.   If Max Reinhardt has been " mainly concerned with extracting the dramatic essence from plays and conveying it as fully as means would admit to the spectator," Meyerhold never did, in spite of what Mr. Carter tells us.   What he did, and still does, is merely to adapt each play to some trick of production or to some idea of a stylised painted or architectural décor or constructions—just as the post-Antoine realistic producers adapt every play to a life-like environment.

After Meyerhold left my sister's Theatre he was engaged at the Imperial Theatres, where his work was very much influenced by one of the best Russian painters, A. Golovin.   When the Soviet Government was more or less firmly established he became a Communist and opened in 1920 his own Theatre in Moscow.   He now produces plays there in a " bio-mechanical " manner, on a bare stage with construc-tions—rostrums and bits of machinery, which are supposed " to symbolise and glorify the mentality of the working classes " in the same way that the luxurious décors of his Imperial production of Molière's " Don Juan," done in the XVII Century " Court manner," were supposed to symbolise and glorify the mentality of the aristocracy.   But the Soviet newspapers are already saying that Meyerhold is following a path which is alien to the Proletarian Theatre, and that his purely intellectual, refined experiments have very little in common with the ideas behind the Workers' Revolution and are com-pletely detached from life.   According to Lenin works of art in a Republic of Workers should be created for Workers and in such a form as to be understandable to them.   Lenin was against Futurism, for instance, considering it not only incomprehensible to the masses, but " even a backward form of art on account of the ideas on which it was based."

After Meyerhold left the Dramatic Theatre my sister asked me to go on with the production of " The Devil's Show " and then engaged N. Evreinov, a talented modern producer, who had to share the work of staging the plays with me and with a former assistant of Meyerhold, A. Zonov. To obtain the money for the following season she was obliged, much against her will, to accept an offer to go to New York with her own Russian company in the spring of 1908. I accompanied her on that tour and was an impotent witness of a great financial debacle, mainly because her managers were a couple of hopeless fools who knew about as much of theatrical conditions in America as of the life of the Tibetan Dalai Lama! She returned to Petersburg quite broken and with very little money left. Still, we succeeded in finding the necessary capital and in starting another (1908-1909) season in her Theatre, but the fatal blow was dealt by the " Most Holy Synod," a kind of Imperial State Ministry of the Russian Orthodox Church. This conclave of Bishops, after witnessing a public rehearsal, had unexpectedly brought about the withdrawal, on the grounds of blasphemy, of Oscar Wilde's " Salome," produced by Evreinov. They had no legal right of interference, as the play had been passed previously by the Censor, but such was the strange state of affairs in Tzarist Russia, that Institutions like the Police and the Church were privileged to act illegally when they

G

wished to do so.   As a great deal of money had been
spent on the production of " Salome " (which was
justified by unusually heavy advance booking) there
was practically nothing left of the Theatre capital, and
my sister decided, after a struggle, to close the Theatre
at the beginning of February, 1909, and once again
went on tour in the provinces in an effort to recover
financially.   But this time it was not with the intention
of re-opening her Theatre.   In a conversation with
me she said that she did not see the possibility of a
Theatre as she had imagined it, unless she could have a
company of actors, united by the same understanding
of the art of acting, who would be able to *feel* each
other when acting together.   She came to the conclusion—to which in their time came Antoine,
Stanislavsky, Eleonora Duse, Copeau and my humble
self, that a Theatre of ideas needs interpreters who
have been brought up on the ideas and on the methods
of that particular Theatre.   Every such Theatre must
be like a community, following a " master," something like what in the art of painting is called a
" school," in which all the disciples carry out freely
and enthusiastically the ideas of their leader and are
able to work all together on the same picture.   My
sister told me that before re-starting a Theatre of her
own she wanted to open a school to prepare her
actors.   As regards herself as an actress she said that
she could not imagine herself acting as a star-actress,
separated from the rest of the production, nor could
she bear to act in a Theatre, the ideas of which had

become alien to her. Under these circumstances, she could not accept the offers which she had received either to tour the provinces again, or to return to the Imperial Theatres or to join the Moscow Art Theatre, and she decided, for the time being, to give up the stage. Speaking of her school to one of her future collaborators, she said that she "would not teach acting there." It was to be "a place in the country, near the sea," where the opportunity would be given to every student " to become a healthy joyful, cultured artist, where all of them together would find out for themselves their own way of acting."

But that dream of an idealist never materialised. The same fate which lay in store for another great actress of our time, Eleonora Duse, whom my sister admired so much, was awaiting her. Like Duse, Vera was an actress of the symbolic Theatre ; like Duse she was an incurably restless seeker " after something in this world which there is no satisfying by half-measure " (Eleonora Duse by Arthur Symonds); like Duse she had "a soul, which was the most beautiful and sensitive instrument imaginable," and like Duse she met an ugly and cruel death.

It is interesting to recall how these two extraordinary women met for the first time. Duse came into Vera's dressing-room with outstretched hands. Vera took them in her own and laid them on her head, and they both stood in silence before each other.

Eleonora Duse was fated to die alone in the blackest and ugliest town in the World, Pittsburg, U.S.A.,

" hell with one lid off," as Henry Irving said, " la plus hideuse ville du monde," as Duse herself asserted on her death bed.   Vera also died alone while on tour far away from her family and friends, beyond the Caspian Sea, in an Asiatic town Tashkent, stricken by an ugly disease, small pox, which she caught amongst the Turkomen in Samarkand, the ancient capital of Tamerlaine and Ghenghiz-Khan.   Poor little sister ! How she had always dreaded the thought of becoming ugly !   I remember once, after a performance, we were sitting together on a large couch in her Study before the fire in our old house in Petersburg at the corner of the " English Perspective."   She was so fond of the brown tiled Dutch fireplace in this room that she wanted to take it with her if she ever had to leave that house, or if that were impossible to smash it with a hammer, " so that nobody else should have it." She told me then that although she was very often tempted to doubt herself, yet somewhere, deep down within her, she had complete faith in her life and calling.   " Nothing will ever make me lose courage and despair except becoming ugly."

During her illness she never lost courage and struggled to the last.   Like Duse, Rejane and Sarah Bernhardt, Vera remained an actress and worked until the moment when her physical strength failed her. She acted night after night with high temperature, until she fell prostrate in the wings after making her final exit.   It is remarkable how much a real actress can endure for the sake of her work and how strong

in her can be the sense of duty.   By a strange coin-
cidence, on that final night of her career, Vera acted the
gay part of the girl " Rosie " in Sudermann's " Battle
of Butterflies "—the same part which had brought her
into the front rank of famous actresses.   She was
taken to her hotel, totally unable to make the slightest
movement, as her skin was coming away in large
flakes from her fragile body.   She bore her sufferings
until the last moment hoping against hope, but died in
a few days on the 10th of February, 1910.

The money which was left after her death was
scarcely enough to pay for her funeral.   Besides
spending nearly everything she had earned in her
Theatre, she was extraordinarily generous and had
never refused to help different organisations for the
assistance of poor students, teachers, actors, Jews
suffering from pogroms, political prisoners, exiles,
etc.   She was always ready even after having played a
most exhausting part to rush to perform at a charity
concert.   During the Revolution of 1905–1906 her
house was a refuge for different people sought after
by the Tzarist Police, amongst whom was the President
of the first Soviet the socialist-menshevik Chroustalev-
Nossar.   When he came with his friend to Vera's
house she did not even know who he was.   I remember she made me shave his fair beard off and cut
his long hair so as to make him unrecognisable to
the Police.   The poor man's appearance was not
improved by my operation.

When Vera's coffin was brought from Tashkent to

Petersburg the crowd was big enough to fill Trafalgar Square, the Strand and Whitehall, yet now they write to me from Russia saying that the public has almost forgotten her.   I could not join the funeral procession until it reached the cemetery, and following from a distance along the Nevsky Prospect I remembered how Vera had sometimes jokingly given me imitations of herself when dead being taken along the same Nevsky Prospect to be buried, and of me walking behind.

Vera's work undoubtedly left strong after-effects on the Russian Theatre.   Whoever her collaborators were and whatever their talents and mistakes may have been—the producers Meyerhold, Evreinov, Zonov and myself, her literary advisers, the critic Akim Volinsky, the poets Valery Bryusov, Alexander Blok, J. Baltroushaytis, the artists Leon Bakst, Alexandre Benois, M. Doboujinsky, Soudekine, N. Sapounov, V. Denisov, Kalmakov, Anisfeld and others—every one of these worked for one idea :—the "theatralisation" of the Theatre.   They all tried to place the imagination in supreme authority in the Theatre and to find purely "theatrical" forms of expression. Her Theatre showed us that the bigger the ideas of a play, the more detached from actuality their expressions should be.   In her Theatre we saw that an actor's business is to create synthetic conditional characters with movements and intonations as demanded by the imaginative form of the play.

All the modern Russian tendencies in the Theatre

"Romeo and Juliet." Moscow, 1921. Tairov.

have resulted from and evolved directly or indirectly from my sister's Theatre.

The painted sets of the artists who led Meyerhold were transformed by other artists like Yakoulov and Exter, who influenced another modern leading Russian producer, Tairov (who started as an actor in Vera's Theatre), into three dimensional cubistic sets and subsequently by still other artists into constructions instead of sets, but the principal aim of all the important Russian producers of later years, Tairov, Vachtangov, Evreinov, Diaghileff, and others, has been the same, *i.e.*, the " theatralisation " of the show.

In western Europe the anti-realistic methods of production were first put into practice in certain small Theatres (at the " Théâtre de l'Oeuvre " of Lugné Poe, for instance), and occasionally in experimental productions of the big Theatres (Reinhardt's for instance). In 1908, however, Georg Fuchs opened his Munchener Kuenstler Theatre of stylised productions and his work was later evolved in Germany into " expressionism." In Paris, in 1912, Jacques Copeau opened the " Vieux Colombier " and had in this theatre a permanent " built " setting, which was an embryo of the later " constructive " settings. His work was followed and advanced upon (after he had been obliged to close his Theatre) by Charles Dullin at the Atelier, by Louis Jouvet, Georges Pitoeff, and in Brussels by Jules Delacre at the Theatre du Marais, and others. Only much later did the anti-realistic movement reach

U.S.A., where it greatly influenced the so-called Little Theatres of the amateurs. Although one of the initiators of the anti-realistic movement was an Englishman, Gordon Craig, whose writings have had an enormous influence on the Theatre all over the world, the movement has never gained any foothold in the English Theatre. This still remains under the influence of realism—not that of Antoine, but of a kind of stagey pretty chocolate box reproduction of life—and false romanticism, and any un-realistic experiments including those of Craig himself are regarded in England as " highbrow," " unusual " and outlandish.

To return to myself—while working in my sister's Theatre I did not think of taking up producing professionally, although I had always been very interested in the Theatre, had read everything I could about it and had seen most of the great actors and the outstanding productions all over the world. I was especially interested in the Opera—probably because I had lived with it since my childhood, as my father was a tenor, firstly in the Italian Opera and then at the Petersburg Imperial Theatre, an idol of the public, and subsequently a professor of the Operatic class at the Moscow Imperial Conservatoire. I had been studying in a Military Academy, where I had been sent by my mother, because she did not consider me sufficiently disciplined, and thought I showed signs of being too fond of freedom. It was well run, like the majority of Russian military schools at that time, mainly because

THEODORE P. KOMISARJEVSKY
(Di Pietro)   My Father

the Grand Duke Constantin Constantinovich, an uncle of the Tzar, was at the head of them. Besides being a general, and President of the Academy of Science, he was a poet, a dramatist and a cultured and liberal-minded man. Sometime I may write a book on my turbulent childhood, when I shall be able to say more about that tall, thin Duke, who, fortunately for him, died before the Revolution, thus escaping the tragic fate of his family. He was very popular among the cadets and had a great influence, not only moral, but also artistic, on all of us. About twenty-five per cent of my comrades did not remain in the army, but became artists, musicians, poets and actors. My ambition at that time was to become an architect. I worked with that object when supervising the artistic side of my sister's Theatre and when I started to produce for her. Although I grew to like theatrical work I never came to feel, as the majority of stage people do, that " the stage is my life," and that " I couldn't live without it." Working for the stage was to me just as exciting as every other work which I had learned and liked, such as—architecture, music, drawing, writing, etc. I loved life itself, and that love for life gave me the energy for work and relief from it, and made it possible for me to see that which was false and poor and stale in my own work as well as in the work of others. I accepted my first job of supervising the artistic side of my sister's Theatre, mainly because I wanted to help her, but also because I had been studying things that qualified me for it and

was keen on learning.   Later, when my sister told me
that I could produce plays, and indeed that she wanted
me to do so, I consented, because I had confidence in
her and felt that it was important for her Theatre at
that moment when it was without a producer that I
should do so.   Personal artistic vanity had nothing to
do with my taking up work in my sister's Theatre.   I
had not the slightest desire to become a stage celebrity
—probably because I had seen so many of them since
my childhood.   When I started producing at the
" Dramatic Theatre " I did not even want to have my
name on the programme, and for quite a long time I
was known in the theatrical circles of Petersburg only
as " Komisarjevsky's brother."   This I must confess,
began to hurt my young " amour propre d'artiste "
when I started to produce on my own.

Besides the play by Remizov already mentioned, I
produced in my sister's Theatre Andreyev's " Black
Masks," Grillparzer's " Ahnfrau," a one act pastoral
with songs by Gluck " The Queen of May," which
had to be given in the same bill with the withdrawn
" Salome," Rachilde's " Madame la Mort," Oscar
Wilde's " The Florentine Tragedy," Hebbel's
" Judith," Goldoni's " Locandiera," Ibsen's " Master
Builder " and the " Doll's House."   For the " Locandiera " J. used backings of chintz stretched on a
frame as scenery of a different pattern and colour
for each act.   The " Doll's House " I produced
in brown folded curtains hanging at an angle.
My sister acted in the last five plays, singing the

"Coq d'Or," by Rimsky Korsakov. Setting for the first act. 1923. Komisarjevsky.

part of the Shepherd in "The Queen of May."
When she went on her last tour I was quite unexpectedly asked to produce Bernard Shaw's "Cæsar
and Cleopatra" in a Petersburg private Theatre, and
this was my first separation from my sister's productions. Later I started in collaboration with N.
Evreinov "The Gay Theatre" with a repertoire of
amusing one-act plays, mostly musical. Amongst
other things we produced Sûppe's operetta "Die
schöne Galathea," Pergolesi's "La Serva Padrona,"
and a skit on the XIXth century vaudeville, "The
Phrenologist." After Vera's death I was, again quite
unexpectedly, appointed permanent producer of the
Moscow Nezlobin Dramatic Theatre where I remained for three years from the autumn of 1910 at a
salary of £300 a year. I gradually gave up the idea of
doing any other work apart from the Theatre, although
I must say that I have always been very grateful to the
fate which made me learn how to do other work. My
knowledge of architecture, painting, music and
literature has proved most useful, not only in my productions, but also as a means of earning money during
those frequent "out of work" periods in the land of
the commercial Theatre.

At the Nezlobin Theatre I began with the production of a tragi-comic play by the Russian classic
Ostrovsky, called "Not a farthing and suddenly a
sixpence"—a sort of Russian "Avare." I did not
treat the play in the traditional manner of the Moscow Imperial Little Theatre, which was considered

Ostrovsky's home, and was like the Comédie Francaise in connection with the productions of Moliere, or the Festival Theatre at Stratford-on-Avon, or the Old Vic as regards the productions of Shakespeare, *i.e.*, the only place that existed or ever could exist for the correct interpretation of Ostrovsky. I did not produce this play as a comedy of mid-nineteenth century suburban middle-class manners, but gave the story and the characters a wider human significance, raising the dramatic situations of the play to tragic heights and broadening the comedy parts. The scenic side of my production was no longer a mere reproduction of a sordid Moscow courtyard, but was treated as an imaginative romantic coloured print. I conceived the place where the story occurred as having once been a wealthy estate on the outskirts of Moscow, long since abandoned by its owners. The old white plastered 18th century lodge, falling into ruins, was on the right of the stage. From there a high fence ran round the back of the stage with a wooden gate through it and a stall-shop in the centre ; behind the fence through the old trees was a glimpse of the roofs of Moscow and a church, silhouetted against the blue summer sky with heavy white clouds. I had the idea of drawing a contrast between the tragic and grotesque events of people's lives and the placid beauty of nature. Besides, I wanted to express by the décors and the costumes the style in which the play was written. The production was successful with the public, but I was very depressed on reading in one of the papers—I used to take press notices very much to heart in those days—that " there is enough stupidity in every wise man " and " that to be the young brother of a great actress does not justify a man in despising all traditions and in distorting a classic on the stage of a Theatre, and that too standing opposite the home of that classic." Unfortunately for me it happened that the Imperial Little Theatre was on the other side of the same square in which the Nezlobin Theatre stood.

During my three years at that Theatre I produced, on an average, a new play every month. Amongst my big productions were the first part of Goethe's " Faust," " Le Bourgeois Gentilhomme " by Moliére, Carlo Gozzi's " Turandot," and my own adaptation of Dostoyevsky's " Idiot." In the production of " Turandot " I successfully applied the principles of the Commediadell' Arte :—the interpreters of the comic characters improvised their parts, talked to the audience, sang, danced, produced acrobatic tricks, and played, to use the latest term of Meyerhold, in the " bio-mechanical " manner.

I applied the same principles in my production of Mr. Arnold Bennett's play " The Bright Island " in London. Although the play seemed to me very interesting and my production, according to the author, expressive of it, the whole thing met with a cold reception. There was, of course, no gagging or improvising as Mr. Bennett had written the spoken text.

" The Idiot " at the Nezlobin Theatre was produced by me without sets, thus anticipating the " set-less " production of " The Karamazovs " at the Moscow Art Theatre. Substituting the settings with mere suggestions of the surroundings I wanted to bring the actors into prominence and to concentrate the attention of the audience on the inner tragic conflicts of Dostoyevsky's people. His big novels seemed to me to be for Russia what the tragedies of Aeschylus had been for Greece, their main theme being the eternal fight between the forces of Christ and Antichrist, and I tried to express that in the production of " The Idiot," Just as later on in London in my production of Hugh Walpole's " The Man with Red Hair " I did not show the horror of the perversity of Crispin to thrill the audience, but in order to reveal his inner conflict between good and evil—so when producing " The Idiot " I wanted to convey Dostoyevsky's idea of redemption and purification through suffering.

The action of the play started in darkness, as though it were the continuation of something which had already happened just as the novel itself begins. First, only a window of the railway carriage appeared lighted from behind, and then the figures of the two men sitting on both sides of it. In the following scenes I had only one plain back-cloth and different sets of furniture necessary for the action ; each scene was lighted according to its mood, and the lights were arranged in such a way that all the settings seemed to be surrounded by a semi-circular frame of darkness. The

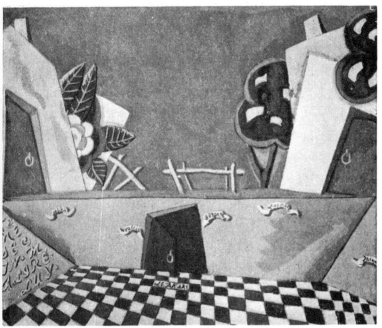

PERMANENT SETTING FOR MOLIERE'S " LE MEDECIN MALGRE LUI."
Komisarjevsky.

garden was suggested by a bench and a backing made of threadbare green sack-cloth hung so that the uneven folds gave an impression of trees, and the spaces between them, with steel blue lights behind, of misty depth.

I left the Nezolbin Theatre in 1913 to work simultaneously in the Moscow Imperial Grand Opera House and in the same Little Theatre, whose traditions I had been violating on the other side of the Square.   I was greeted in the Imperial Theatres in the same way as every other " intruder," that is, everyone did his best to force me to work in their traditional manner or to get rid of me as quickly as possible. My first production in The Little Theatre in 1913 was Molière's " Le Medicin Malgré-Lui."   I had one permanent set for all the three acts of this farce, a special proscenium arch with boxes in it and a special front drop curtain.   The musicians, dressed in costumes, sat in these boxes.   I conceived the production in the manner of the French XVIIth century Fair shows with Lully's music, and dancing, to blend rhythmically with the text of the play.   The actors were dressed in the stylised costumes of the characters of the Théâtre de la Foire—Gros Guillaume, Turlupin, etc., and played as in a buffonade.   The first rehearsals at the " Little Theatre " were even more trying than my first rehearsal at my sister's Theatre, but this time I put my " amour propre d'artiste " in my pocket and showed such self-possession, that one of the " pillars " who was used to temperamental producers exclaimed in exasperation—" That young fellow is an Englishman and not a producer ! " The first night of my production was to have been on the anniversary of the birth or death—I don't remember which—of Stchepkin, a celebrated Russian actor-realist, who was a sort of idol of The Little Theatre, and who, as the " pillars " of The Little Theatre assured me, used to act the part of Sganarelle realistically in the same play seventy years ago. After the dress rehearsal I was called to the office of the General Manager of The Little Theatre, who was a famous actor as well as a prince, and, was informed much to my surprise that although my production was " very interesting and might be representative of the *future* of The Little Theatre, it was neither representative of its past nor its present and therefore it would not possibly do for the anniversary and must be postponed." It would undoubtedly have been postponed indefinitely, had not something been done by the Director in the matter (he probably telephoned from Petersburg to say that he wanted to see my production)—which resulted in the play being done the day after the anniversary, when nearly everyone in the cast hoped and prayed that it would be a failure. However, they were doomed to disappointment ; the Director was well satisfied, and so was the public. The leading comedian, who played Sganarelle, was so chagrined at the applause that on the way to his dressing-room after the last call, he threw his " beret " on the ground exclaiming: "Damn the suckling ! "—meaning me.

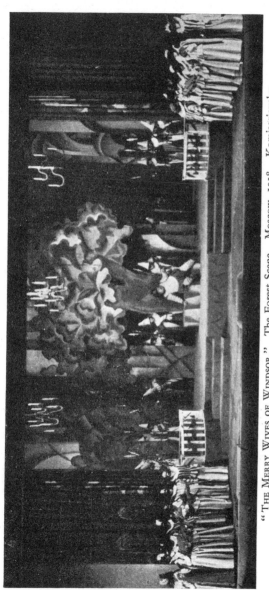

"The Merry Wives of Windsor." The Forest Scene. Moscow, 1918. Komisarjevsky.

At the Imperial Opera I was given the following to produce : " Sadko " by Rimsky Korsakov, " Eugene Onyeguin " by Chaikovsky, " Manon Léscaut " by Puccini, Wagner's " Parsifal " and " Don Juan " by Mozart. But the ruthless intrigues in both Theatres were too much for me, and finally I decided to leave the Imperial Stage and announced my intention to the Director. He, however, declared that it was mere weakness on my part and that he had hoped that I was going to " bite through the windpipes of the old brigade."

But I resigned and made a contract as artistic director and chief producer with Ziminne the owner of the Private Moscow Opera House, a large building with an auditorium bigger than that of the Imperial Opera. Ziminne, a fat man with grey curly hair, looked like a cardinal, but was as obstinate and wilful as a child albeit kind hearted and generous towards his collaborators. He had strange fancies—for instance, he liked all his producers, conductors, scenic artists and favourite singers to go with him after the show in a party to the " Russian Baths "—but he did very good work in his Theatre, and quite a number of the best Russian operatic artists started their careers under his management. The only artistic draw-back of this institution was that Ziminne took the liberty of lighting the sets of every production himself. This was done by means of a telephone installed in his private box opposite the stage, and he kept the electricians in constant terror, as he even changed the lighting during the performances and often assured them that they had made

H

a mistake, even when they had not. My most important productions at this Theatre were :— Borodin's " Prince Igor," for which I devised the groupings, costumes and sets in the style of the old ikons, Moussorgsky's " Boris Godounov," S. I. Taneiev's " Oresteya " (after the tragedy of Aeschylus) and a very interesting experiment in realistic opera— " Klara Militch " written by Kastalsky and based on Tourgueniev's story of the same name. Later, when Ziminne's Opera became the Soviet Opera House, I remained there in the same capacity. In 1918 I returned as Director to the former Imperial Grand Theatre, still remaining the Director of the Soviet Opera House.

In 1910, while at the Nezlobin Theatre, I started in a basement of my friend's house a School of the Theatre, to which I added in 1914 a small experimental Studio-Theatre in memory of my sister. This Studio-Theatre was in a private house where I converted the big drawing-room into an auditorium for 160 people. There, I produced Aristophanes' " Lysistrata," Hofmannsthal's " Electra," Van Lerberghe's " Pan," Hauptmann's " Hannele " and " Everyman." In addition, some works of the modern Russian writers (Andreyev, M. Kouzminn, A. Remizov, F. Sologoub), and my own adaptations of Dickens' " Christmas Carol " (which was the biggest success of the first season), Dostoyevsky's " A Bad Joke," Balzac's " Love under the Mask," and T. Hoffman's " The Choice of the Bride."

In 1918 with the assistance of the " Artistic and
Educational Union of the Worker's Organisations " I
transferred the activities of this Studio Theatre and of
my School to a proper theatrical building, " Theatre
Zon " (which had previously been the home of a
Moscow " Moulin Rouge," where before the Revolu-
tion the rich Muscovites were entertained with
" Wein, Weib, Gesang und Tanz," particularly with
"Wein und Weib"), and where I was producing,
rehearsing, and teaching right up to the day I left
Moscow.

CHAPTER FOUR

An American interview

Hoo ! Hoo ! Hoo—hoo !
Whizzzz . . . .
Dong—dong—dong—dong—dong !
Hoo ! hoo—hooooo . . .
BANG ! BANG !! BANG !!! Bang-bang-bang-bang-BANG !!!!
DONG-DONG-DONG-DONG ! Hoo-hoo !
WHIZZZ ! BANG ! HOO !

This is what I listened to while standing at a window on the trembling floor of a small overheated room on the twenty-first floor of a New York Hotel before a cubist landscape of the roofs of the City. As I gazed at the hooting, clanging and roaring streets below, it seemed to my bewildered mind as if it were some whizzing, whistling, overwound mechanical toy which had gone crazy. I had seen one like it in miniature in the gardens of the Archbishop of Salzburg.

The managers of the "Theatre Guild"—very hospitable, hearty and enthusiastic people—who had invited me to New York from London to produce plays for them, had met me at the quay just at the moment when a friendly customs' official, after patting me on the back and calling me "young feller," had finished turning my trunk inside out and succeeded in smashing the glass in every one of my framed sketches.

I had been escorted to my hotel—which seemed, as the taxi approached it, like a huge tiled Dutch stove—and left in this vibrating room to rest.   This, however, I soon found impossible, and after looking out of the window I had a bath and picked up a newspaper which was given gratis to guests by the considerate management of the hotel.

Some headlines caught my attention :

" STARVATION IN RUSSIA.   PEASANT WOMAN EATING HER CHILDREN " . . . " WIZARD FINANCIER RELEASED FROM JAIL AND WELCOMED TO A FRESH START IN FINANCIAL OPERATIONS " . . . " BROAD-WAY STAR ARRIVES FROM ITALY LOCKED IN A TRUNK " . . .

Just as I came to a headline announcing that " STOCK MARKET " should be " THE CHIEF CONCERN OF AN ART CRITIC," the 'phone rang and I was told the lady reporter of a Magazine wished to interview me downstairs. As I had received instructions from my managers that I must do my utmost to be pleasant to reporters I immediately rushed to the lift and arrived in one fell swoop at the ground floor. In the noisy lounge—marble with copious gilt decorations every-where—I found a pleasant middle-aged, bespectacled lady with hair done like Liszt, wearing a check cloak,

fur hat with a couple of feathers in it, and snow boots.
She shook hands with a smile which is usually described as " charming " or " sweet," and which can be
turned on or off quite independently of the mood in
which the smiler may happen to be.   It is only
necessary to contract the corners of the mouth towards
the ears, and the smile is on, by relaxing the mouth the
smile is off!   Simple and practical !

After smiling at each other " charmingly " we
retired to a quiet (right under the elevated railway)
Gothic drawing-room where the lady produced a note
book and three fountain pens, and the following
conversation took place :

—Would you tell me exactly how you pronounce
your name ?

—Theodore Ko-mi-sar-jev-sky.

—That name will cost me my best compositor yet !
—she remarked as she wrote it down.—You are
Russian ?

—If you like.

—Do you mean that you are not ?

—I mean that I had a Russian passport before the
Revolution, but now we Russians who reside abroad
have become a sort of new gypsy tribe.   We no
longer belong officially to any Nation.   The " League
of Nations " kindly gives us passports which are
supposed to enable us to travel anywhere ("passeport,"
as you know, derives from " passe partout !"), but we
can only enter those countries which graciously agree
to receive us.

—How trying !

—Very.   But I don't object to the idea of being a gypsy.   I love freedom more than anything.   I have always considered myself as a sort of " citoyen de l'univers."   After all, I was born outside Russia.   My father was born in the Ukraine which has been striving for centuries to become independent of Russia.   My mother was a princess.   (I was told not to forget to emphasise this fact to the reporters !)

—Would you tell me her name ?

—Maryia Petrovna Koriatovitch Kourzevitch.

—How cute !   Where did she come from ?

—She was of Polish-Lithuanian origin, a direct descendant of the King Hedimin himself . . .

—Oh, gee !

—One of my great-grandfathers was French, somebody in the family was, I believe, Scotch . . .

—Very unusual !—and she jotted down a note.

—Is it ?   Are you American ?

—Sure !   I was born in the States.

—Were your father and mother American ?

—No, my mother was German and my father Dutch.   Why do you ask ?   Oh, I see what you mean !—She smiled—Nationality is merely a matter of passport, is that it ?

—Not quite.   It is a matter of what one feels oneself to be.   For some people its a matter of habit.

—Do you find our rooms too hot ?—she asked, noticing that I had been wiping the perspiration from my forehead

—I do.

Here she made a note.

—Do you like Americans ?

—I do.

—We love Russians !   But as you said that you weren't Russian . . .

—I am as Russian as you are American.

We smiled charmingly at each other !

—Do you find Americans very different to Europeans ?

—The hectic pace of your life and its jazzy rhythm is a little overwhelming, but I much admire the energy you put into your work.

—Yes, we do things quickly here.

(I had reason to remember her words later, when I fainted beneath the stage during the first night—after rehearsing for a week until five o'clock in the morning —and only came to my senses 48 hours later !)

—Don't you think we are more *artistic* in our Theatre and less commercial than, for example, the English ?

—I think you are more interested in anything new, more international in spirit, more enterprising, and you don't mind taking big risks.   That's why you have an artistic Theatre like The Theatre Guild and that's why your commercial theatre sometimes produces more advanced plays than any other commercial Theatre, but your commercial managers still dominate the Theatre here in the same gambling spirit as anywhere else.

"The Merry Wives of Windsor." The Basket Scene. Moscow, 1918. Komisarjevsky.

—What do you think of the London critics?

—Every actor thinks that a critic is a subtle and marvellous man when he praises the actor's work, but he becomes a horrid ignoramus in the actor's opinion when he ceases to do so. The majority of the London critics have treated my productions in a very appreciative way. Mr. St. John Ervine even wrote to me: " I do not know any critic who is not pleased by your presence in our Theatre, and I trust that you will long continue to remain here."

—Are you personally acquainted with the famous critic?

—I've not had the pleasure of meeting him.

—Are you acquainted with any royalties then? Did you ever meet the Tzar, or Lenin, or any Grand Dukes?

—I did, yes.

—Would you tell me all about them?—She moved eagerly in her chair.—What did the Tzar look like?

—Just a small man with a small beard—in uniform.

—What was Lenin like?

—Just a small man with a small beard and great ideas—without a uniform.

—I see.   Where did you meet Lenin?

—In the street on one occasion, in a room on another.

—And the Tzar?

—I saw him in the street, indoors, and on a railway platform.

—How, on a railway platform? Tell me more about it! Don't be so laconic, please!

—The last time I saw him was on the outbreak of the Revolution when he was trying to reach St. Petersburg from the front.

—Where was it?

—In a small provincial town, a kind of Spa, which happened to be a railway junction. I had gone there for a holiday.

—To get new inspiration for your work amidst nature, lying in the grass—started she poetically.

—We have no grass at the end of February—only snow and mud.

—Of course! I didn't realise that it was February, but please go on!

—One night I was playing cards and drinking tea with a friend with whom I was staying . . .

—Russians always drink tea, don't they?

—Yes.

—It's most thrilling! I am sorry to interrupt you. Do go on!

—As I said, we were drinking tea when a 'phone message came from a friend living near the station, saying that the Imperial train had arrived. We jumped into a cab . . .

—What is a cab in Russian?

—Izvoztchik.

—Oh, gee!

—We took an izvoztchik and drove to the station.

There we saw the Imperial train with its windows ablaze with light and . . .

—With the Tzar and his suite inside !

—No.

—Where was His Majesty then ?

—We noticed a small man in trench coat and grey astrakhan Cossack cap at the far end of the empty platform.   We approached and found it was the Tzar.

—Say kid !   And you spoke to the Tzar ?

—We did not.   We looked at him and he looked at us and a moment later he crossed the line to his train.

—What was His Majesty waiting for ?

—He was trying to get to St. Petersburg from the front, but the railway workers had pulled up the track and he had been obliged to go by a loop line which had also been wrecked.   When he left the station where we saw him he went North to Pskov where in that very train he signed his abdication.

—But where was the Tzar's suite ?

—There wasn't any suite.

—You don't say so !

—Yes, I do.   Except for three or four people everyone left him when they saw the impending danger and later he was deserted by all, and lived a whole year in constant fear of being murdered.

—He must have been in an agony of mind on that platform !

—The station master, who hid himself that night but whom we saw next day, said that the Tzar was drunk.   He may have been lying, I don't know.

—How tragic !

—Very.

She wrote something down and then asked :

—What is your artistic credo ?

—I don't quite understand.

—Well, you have been advertised here as an " expressionist " and . . .

—Oh, I see. I believe it was a publicity stunt. Stanislavsky is coming here with his Moscow Art Theatre and as *he* has been advertised as a realist they had to invent something to make competition, so they've advertised me as an expressionist.

—You are not an expressionist then ?

—I suppose I am one officially if you have been told so, but privately I think, that. . . . Only you mustn't publish what I think or it might get me into trouble.

—What do you take me for ?

—Well then, privately, I think that a theatrical producer, or as you call him here a director, must produce a play in the idiom in which it is written. The producer's business is to *interpret* a play on the stage through the ensemble of actors and with the help of every means of expression which the stage possesses.   A producer who alters a play in order to demonstrate some new theory or trick of production is just a nuisance in the theatre, no better than a selfish " star " actor . . .

—But, as you were advertised as an expressionist— she insisted—would you tell me in a few words something about that " school ? "

—In brief : realism registers objective facts of life and the psychology of those facts—Henry Becque, John Galsworthy, for instance. For an impressionist like Chehov only the facts, expressive of the feelings, are of interest. Expressionism, as understood in Germany (Kaiser, Toller) where that school originated, disregards objective reality altogether, even the reality of an actor, if by doing so the ideas of the playwright or the producer can be more saliently demonstrated. Ough !—and again I wiped my perspiring forehead.

—Now would you tell me something about acting ? What is your theory ?

—I am afraid it would take much too long, and I . .

—I see—she looked at her wrist-watch—it's nearly lunch time.

—Yes, I am lunching with my managers. I have been promised oysters looking like raw beefsteaks and ice-cream with boiling sauces.

—I won't keep you any longer—and she got up. But as my Magazine would be very interested to have your ideas on acting perhaps you would write something for us ? We shall be delighted to publish it.

—I'll try.

—Many thanks.—She shook hands and smiled—I have been so interested in what you have told me, Mr. Ko-Komakicksky ! You have a terribly difficult name !
—Yes, a stage hand in London used to call me " Come and seduce me."

—They have a very quaint sense of humour, the

English—said she without smiling—haven't they? Do you like them?

—Very much.

We both smiled sweetly and she left the room.

The following week I read my interview with her in the magazine.

She had written :

TOO CHILLY FOR THE MOSCOW DIRECTOR.

" THAT THEOPHITE KORMAGENSKY, LATE DIRECTOR OF ALL THE RUSSIAN THEATRES, A PERSONAL FRIEND OF THE LAST TZAR OF RUSSIA AND OF LENIN (GREAT PEOPLE ARE ALWAYS IMPARTIAL !) SHOULD COMPLAIN THAT HIS HOTEL IS TOO COLD IS SURPRISING, AS THE THEATRES WHICH THE EXPRESSIONIST DIRECTOR MANAGED IN THE RUSSIAN CAPITAL WERE ALWAYS UNHEATED. THE MANAGERS WHO BROUGHT HIM OVER HERE TO STAGE THEIR NEW OFFERINGS WILL HAVE TO PUT AN ELECTRIC HEATER IN HIS MAGNIFICENT SUITE AT THE HOTEL IF THEY WANT HIS SERVICES. DIRECTOR KOGMARENSKY DOESN'T LOOK AT ALL AS RUSSIANS USUALLY DO—HE'S BALD AND CLEAN SHAVEN ! INCIDENTALLY, HE TOLD US THAT HIS MOTHER WAS A GYPSY PRINCESS. : . :"

Two weeks later I sent her the following article which, however was never published, because, as she wrote to me, there was not enough topical pep in it.*

---

* I produced in New York, during the winter of 1922–23, A. A. Milne's " The Lucky One," Claudel's " The Tidings Brought Mary," and Ibsen's " Peer Gynt " for the " Theatre Guild."

CHAPTER FIVE

" Personalities " and actors—The importance of imagination in acting—Relaxation—Character acting—The study of a part—The processes of acting—Ensemble acting—Cultivation of the imagination —The actor's physique—Tones and inflections—Systems of acting— " Untheatrical " acting—" Stagey " acting—Stanislavsky's system and Chehov—The " truth " on the stage

" DEAR MADAM "—I wrote to the lady reporter— " assuming that the readers of your magazine, in common with the readers of most other papers, dislike lengthy and uninteresting theories, I have attempted in this article to describe as briefly and undogmatically as possible the art of acting and the processes through which the *good* actor must pass in order to create a living character. Had I written a comprehensive theory on the art of acting, I fear you would have been unable to publish it, as the necessary excursions into the history and psychology of acting would have required a couple of volumes rivalling the ' London Telephone Directory,' and that, as you know, is thick enough to kill anybody.

The art of the Theatre is the art of acting and the *good* Theatre depends firstly on actors. The term " born actor " so often used is very misleading. One naturally assumes that a *good* actor has some latent talent, but nothing can be achieved without the constant training of the mind and body for acting purposes.

The modern theatre, sad to say, requires very little of its " actors." Nowadays, people are frequently engaged to act simply because they look the part. But such engagements do not make out of these people actors and actresses. It is true too that very often it is sufficient to possess what is termed " personality," *i.e.*, an attractive or unusual appearance combined with a certain amount of arrogance, plus certain mannerisms and a dose of " sex appeal " to play even the leading parts in the modern Theatre. Yet again, " personality " alone cannot make its possessor into an actor. There are many things to learn and many other qualities besides those of " type " and " personality " required to become a good actor.

The first essential is *imagination*. The imagination includes the conscious and the sub-conscious mind. Its most intense form in which the sub-conscious prevails is called vision. There are three kinds of imagination—the visual, the aural, and that in which both these are combined. The first creates images in space, the second in time, and the third in both. An actor, who was to use all his physical and psychic powers must possess the third kind of imagination. The other essentials for an actor are strong sensibility, vitality, intelligence, and the power of concentration and hard work. To know *how* to work, an actor must understand what acting is.

Some people think that when an actor represents a character on the stage he is merely imitating himself in his own life or different people seen in life and reproducing the lines and directions of a playwright, colouring them with his " temperament." This is true enough of some actors but not of the good ones. A good actor studies the character he finds in the play in order to *imagine* it and to *transform* himself into it. While acting he lives the life of the character as imagined by himself and feels the words and the actions of the character as his own. When an actor chooses a part for himself he does so because the part interests him, appeals to his sense of self-expression and gives him the desire to become the character of the part. When the actor reads the play his mind begins a complicated process of assimilation. It receives sensations from the play and the part, and these sensations combined with the creative associations of his mind form his perception of the part, and this naturally will be an individual one. During the first rehearsals, the actor concentrates on forming the " image " of the character, as well as the " images " which shall prompt all his actions. His " assimilations " become more and more complicated and transform his first perception. For the purposes of acting, the " image " of the character as well as the " images " prompting his actions, must be sufficiently definite and clear and the emotions roused sufficiently rich (of an assimilative, creative order) to stimulate the actor to sincere outer expression. Hence the more the actor is interested in his part, and the greater his concentration on the imaginative stimulus, the more individual the actor's representation becomes ; that is

I

to say, that a character created by a playwright reflects
in the actor's mind to the extent of his imagination.
As the rehearsals proceed the actor is helped more and
more as he becomes conscious of his projected "images"
—in the movements he makes, in the lines he speaks
(when the character has been consistently conceived
by the playwright), in the stimulus he receives from
the other characters in the play, in his surroundings
and relationship to objects.   And when he feels that
the projections of his " images " are the right ones, an
actor will know at once that he is expressing what he
desires to express, and this will excite him to further
efforts until he feels himself completely in accord with
the character his imagination has assimilated.

The ability of an actor to transform himself into the
character imagined by him depends largely upon his
emotional capacities and reactions, but his intelligence
directs and controls his work.   The process of
imagining includes the intelligence and the will power
as well as the emotions.   When an imaginative actor
is on the stage his intellect controls his acting without
the necessity for him to watch himself from the
outside as some theorists (Diderot for instance)
suggest.   When he is playing a part, he believes in the
reality of the " phantoms " imagined by him, but at the
same time never loses sight of the fact that those
" phantoms " are but the objects of his " jeu."   If he
did, he would become the victim of hallucination, *i.e.*,
the *object* would be the master of the *subject* and his
performance would cease to be an act of imaginative

COSTUME FOR SHERIDAN'S "DUENNA." Produced in 1923 at the "Comédie des Champs Elysées," Paris. Komisarjevsky.

creation, in which the artist remains the master. While playing, he actively and definitely registers that which belongs to his " jeu " and is expressive of the character, but at the same time he remains passively aware of the fact that he is only acting. For an imaginative actor to become *actively* aware of, for instance, the audience, the footlights, people in the wings, or to call to mind anything not directly concerned with the character he is playing, would be as good as to stop acting. If he were to " jump " out of his part by becoming actively aware of any of these things he would have to rid his mind of them before being able to act again. Instead of merely simulating, he would have to make his mind a blank, relax his body, and then concentrate his thoughts on that moment of his character's activity at which he had lost it.

An actor should always relax before going on the stage in order to allow full scope for the play of his imagination. Although a comedian once assured me that he always acted much better after quarrelling with his wife, it was not thinking of the row which made him act well, but rather anticipating a pleasant job, which enabled him to forget the unpleasant experience of actual life. If he had not temporarily forgotten the row with his wife he would never have been able to act as well as he did.

Macready, it is said, used to whisper under his breath and swing a ladder violently in the wings before going on the stage. A comedian I knew was in the habit of roundly cursing himself before giving his turn.   Ermolova, a famous Russian tragic actress, always stood waiting her entrance cue with her head bowed or covered with a shawl and would allow no one to speak to her.   On the other hand I knew a tragedian who would insist on telling funny stories before going on to play the last scene as Othello. These things were done in order to free the mind from distracting thoughts.

I usually give my students a simple exercise which I would recommend for every day use to all those " constipated " players, who, when acting allow their muscles to contract in such a way that no emotion can get through at all.   The student sits on a chair, makes his mind a blank and relaxes his body ; after a minute or two, he must look at something, for example the back of his chair, to *see* its shape and colour ; then he must touch it, to *feel* whether it is cold, polished or rough etc.   This exercise is not only very useful for the purpose of relaxing, but for the development of the power of concentration, without which nothing can be imagined on the stage.

To explain the work of an actor and the process of acting let us take a scene in which the actor is playing a man who enters a room unexpectedly and finds his wife whom he loves, lying unconscious on a couch with her dress torn.

To play that scene the actor must know exactly what sort of *character* he has to represent.   When he acts from a written play, he finds the character by

studying the play.   When there is no written play and
the actor has to improvise, he must himself invent all
those images which are to make him act the character.

I must make it clear to the reader that by " acting a
character" I do not mean what is very often understood
on the stage by " character acting " :—*i.e.*, to represent someone who squints or who speaks with
a lisp, to use an assumed voice or an accent, to
appear in an odd make-up or make grotesque or
eccentric gestures.   The appearance and the outer
expressions are reflections in the actor's physique of
the inner life of the character.   The actor imagines
these reflections and perfects them while rehearsing,
but does not assume them as he would, for instance,
put on a borrowed suit or a cardboard nose, of
which he is conscious all the time.   To act a character
means first of all to express its inner life by action.   I
have heard people assert that Duse was *not an actress*,
because " she always remained herself " and very
seldom changed her appearance.   In the first place—if
these same people had seen her play Juliet in Shakespeare's play, they would be obliged to admit they
were wrong.   When I saw her in that part she was
over thirty.   In the wings she looked, with lines in
her face and a stern expression, even more than her
age, but immediately she began to act, she became a
naive, smiling child with a young voice and girlish
gestures.   Secondly—Duse did not use much make-up
because she knew that it marred the subtle play of
expression on her sensitive features.

I remember on one occasion watching Tommaso Salvini in the wings. He was waiting to go on in the Senate scene in " Othello," and stooping like the old man of seventy that he was at that time. But as he made his entrance he became taller and younger and more upright—he was no longer Salvini but Othello in spite of the fact that he did not assume any " theatrical " characteristic attitude—and on the stage his voice, the voice whose accents were so old and tired in the dressing room, sounded young and vigorous.

Sarah Bernhardt played young women when nearly eighty. Of course, since she looked a physical wreck it was at times ridiculous, but there were moments even in the most grotesque performances, when it was possible to forget her age and believe in her acting, because Sarah Bernhardt even at eighty was capable of *feeling* herself young. The young make-up merely made her less convincing. She should have appeared without any and left her looks to our imagination. I did not see " la divine Sarah " when she was younger but if I am to believe one of her critics, a man whom I knew to possess very good taste and judgment, she looked eighteen when playing Joan of Arc at sixty. " What do I care about her real age " —said he—" I give her as much as I can from the front. I go to the Theatre not to marry an actress but to get the illusion, and if I get it I am satisfied. To play young girls at the age of sixty is a special feature of Sarah's talent."

The study of a play for the purpose of finding the

"The Merry Wives of Windsor." The proscenium. Moscow, 1918. Komisarjevsky.

character should be divided into three stages, although each of these stages usually includes some of the work that has to be done during the others. Each of these three stages of the actor's work on a part demands *concentration*. The first stage consists of the un- prejudiced reading of the play to obtain a spontaneous perception of it. The second : the analysis of the play and of the part. Thirdly : the synthesis, in which everything the actor has learnt in the first two stages is put together and expressed in the acting. An actor should never start to study merely from analysis of his part because it weakens his sensibility to it, which is essential to his transformation into the character. " L'intélligence "—said Talma—" n'agit qu'après la sensibilité ; elle juge les impressions, que nous fait éprouvir celle-ci, elle les choisis, les ordonne."

Joseph Kainz, one of the great actors of the Con- tinental Theatré, wrote in his diary as regards the first stage in the study of a part :—" Jede Rolle ist als ein Teil eines in sich geschlossenen Ganzen zu betrachten, zu behandeln und darzustellen." " To be able to understand a part," he says, " a thorough knowledge of the whole play is essential. This cannot be achieved without concentration. With an open mind one begins to read. Scene after scene passes before one's eyes until the end. One *sees* them without listening to the *understanding*. After reading the play in this way, put it aside and await from the depth of one's soul that true clearness of perception and assimilation which leads to creative art—den Beginn des Befrûchtungs und Gebûrtsaktes."

During the second stage of his work on a part the actor must concentrate on the analysis of his character's life and of the psychology of his action, on the meaning, rhythm and style of the character's lines, on the sequence of his actions, and on the relations of his character to the other characters in the play etc.

During the third he concentrates essentially on " acting " his character—*i.e.* on such " images " of the events, of people, of objects, of the surroundings of the past, present and future life of the character, which prompt the actor's words, silences and movements on the stage.

As the life of a human being is continuous, without intervening gaps, the acting of an actor on the stage must be continuous, and all the " images " in his mind which make him desire to speak and do things must be linked together in one unbroken sequence. The actor must have that continuity definitely fixed in his mind during the third stage of his work, so as to be able to avoid thinking of it while acting. During the performance the flow of " images " in response to the actor's will, moves automatically in his mind and prompts him to act.

During the third stage of his work an actor also *perfects* all his means of expression—intonations inflections, gestures and movements—and stylizes them according to the requirements of the style of the play and of its production.

Let us return to our scene of the husband finding his wife and presume that our actor has already conceived in his mind the character he is to represent.   On entering, he must " react " to what he sees.   But in order to react to what the *character* sees, the actor must already *be* the character at the moment of entrance. He will have to imagine some " image " before entering by which he is able to get himself into the mood in which the character has to make his entrance. It is thus clear that acting does not start only at the moment of appearing on the stage.   If our actor is to be light-hearted on entering, he has to imagine before entering something which will *make* him gay. If for instance, the fact of buying an evening paper and finding that he has won a bet on a race can produce the desired effect he must concentrate on that fact and then he will feel pleasure and the desire to express that pleasure in his acting.   As he loves his wife (to feel love for her, he must visualise her and all the facts which make him love her), and as they are poor (to get the feeling of being poor he must visualise facts illustrative of his poverty), he desires to tell her of his good luck.   With that desire and in light-hearted mood he enters.   The carrying of the newspaper in his hand and the actual opening of the door will help him to act the scene.   The sight of his wife lying on the couch, of her " image "—of her face, her attitude— will make him react, *i.e.* will change his mood and awaken in him the desire to act according to his new mood.   To act sincerely he must actually see her, he must let her image sink into his mind, and to do that he must concentrate on her. If nothing interferes—since there is no one else in our scene and nothing else to attract his attention the registration of which would make him think and wish differently—his desire on seeing his wife will be solely connected with the image of his wife. Starting to act in the way he desires, our actor will register new " images " which will awaken in him the desire to continue acting. If, according to the plot, his wife turns out to be dead, the actor, looking at her eyes, has to concentrate on the thought that they look lifeless. Then the desire will rise in him to be certain as to whether or no she is dead. Feeling her forehead with his hand, he will have to concentrate on the thought that it is cold, the realisation of which will lead to other actions, such as, for instance, rushing to the telephone, calling somebody, or crying etc.

If, according to the plot, our actor has to discover that his wife is not dead but has only fainted, then, feeling her forehead, he must conceive it as being warm, concentrating on which will result in a desire to see her move, talk, etc., and he will act accordingly. If his wife should move, the actor must register every movement, which will arouse fresh desires in him for other actions. If she says anything, he must actually listen to her words and let them sink into his mind and they, like her movements, will react on him in such a way as to produce both actions and words.

From this it is clear that when acting with one or

more partners, action or movement should be prompted
not only by the " images " created in one's own mind,
as happen if acting alone, but also by the " images "
and actions of one's partners.   An imaginative actor
must actually listen to his partner, when he is supposed to hear him, look at him, and actually see him,
when he is supposed to see him and not merely
" catch the cues " or look somewhere above the other
person's forehead or stare into the audience, and
make a facial expression as all the bad actors do.
Vera Komisarjevsky used to say that if an actor " not
only feels every word he says himself, but also everything said to him or round him by others, he will be
surprised to find how much deeper and more brilliant
his acting will become, and what is more important—
how much warmer ! "

By saying " actually see his partner " I mean that the
imaginative actor must see his partner as he wants
to see him for the purposes of his acting.   He trans-
forms him in his imagination, assimilating his pre-
sentation of the part with his own conception of it
during the rehearsals ; he makes his partner the object
of his " jeu."

In addition to the fact that the whole cast must
be united by a common understanding of the play
and its production, team-work or the " ensemble "—
without which there can be no scenic interpretation of a play—is possible only if the players are
innerly connected with each other.   Even when,
according to the plot, an actor in an ensemble-

scene is not interested in his partners and not listening
to or looking at them, and his thoughts are focussed
on such " images " in his mind which enable him
to behave as a separate unit, his acting must still be
in keeping with the mood and the general idea of
the scene, and he must be prepared to resume the
inner contact with his partners at the appointed
moment.

If, for instance, an actor " A " starts a scene alone,
then we may say that he and all the objects of his
" jeu " are enclosed in the small circle of his
imaginary life, which is surrounded by a larger
circle, representative of the interpretation of the
whole play. If another character, " B," enters
and they are not interested in each other, they are,
as it were, each in two separate circles of imaginary
activity.   When they get into contact with and
look at and listen to each other, they are enclosed in
one circle, either in one of " A," if " B " is interested
in " A," or in one of " B," if " A " is interested in
" B."   If a third character, " C," enters and
immediately comes into contact only with " B,"—let
us suppose he does not know " A," and is not
interested in him—then : if " A " is not interested
in " C " and does not wish to listen to what " B "
and " C " are saying or doing, he will remain within
his own circle, while " B " and " C " will be within
their circle, or, if " A " is interested in   " B "
and " C," he will remain in their circle, let us say
until " C," who does not want " A " to listen, takes

" B " out of it.   This roughly indicates " ensemble "
acting.

In a production in which the actors are not in
direct communication with the audience they should
not include the latter in the circles of their imagination
A, B, C, etc.   When an actor has to be in communication with the audience (as happens in some
unrealistic plays, and in certain " conditional " productions) the audience must be included in the circles
A, B, C, etc., and its reactions must be registered and
answered by the players.

In the foregoing scene the " ensemble " acting—
although in the first version the wife is supposed to
be dead and immovable—must start the moment the
husband sees her.   The actress playing the wife must
help the husband to act by her position on the couch,
her face and the detail of her dress.   In the second
version, in which the wife is alive, all her movements
and words must be registered and felt by the husband
and *vice versa*.   The actions of the one must stimulate
the imagination and be answered by the reactions of
the other.

To be able to play our improvised scene without
the feelings of the actors running away with them—
since there is no definite detailed form, as in a written
play, the details and the continuity of the story must
be thought out and planned beforehand by both actors
and then put into definite shape during rehearsals.

Highly emotional actors playing that scene in the
way I suggest will be more intense and moving than

actors of the "thinking" type, but both will be convincing and true because they are not simulating but concentrating their minds on such "images" as will evoke reactions both real and essential to the situation.

It is unnecessary to say that none of these reactions are possible unless the imagination and physique of the actor are trained.

The cultivation of the imagination is helped by keeping free from the conventionalities of the stage and all the stereotyped forms, habits and mannerisms connected with it and by keeping in touch with real life in all its variety and with all the other stimulating forms of art. An actor should study not only those parts which he plays, but also those which appeal to him apart from the chance of ever acting them. He must also perform exercises to develop and perfect his power of concentration, his reactions, his spontaneity, his presence of mind and inventive faculty. These exercises should consist of improvisations of short scenes such as I have already given, with or without words. Scenes without words, or "mimes," should sometimes be acted with music as exercises. The actor chooses a piece of music, invents a story to fit the form of the music, and acts it. When I speak of "mimes" I am not suggesting anything in the style of the classic ballet dancing, or "plastic" exercises, or barefoot "Greek" dancing. The actor must act in mime just as in a play. The only difference between acting in dumb show and in musical mime lies

Setting for Alfano's "Madonna Imperia." Teatro di Torino, 1927. Komisarjevsky.

in the fact that in the latter every action and its continuity must fit into the music's form and time and the
rhythm of the actor's movements must be in keeping
with the rhythm of the music.   Exercises of this sort
are essential for the development of rhythmical sensibility, which will enable the actor's bodily movements
to work in simultaneous co-operation with his mind
so that his physique may become a sensitive " baro-
meter " of his feelings.

"Der Korper des modernen Schauspielers ist ein
Reagent, das Instrument, auf dem die Motive spielen "
—said Kainz.   " The movements of the actor's body
are the expression of the *Psyche*, the external signs of
what is happening within.   As the sea moves slightly
even in calm weather and affords us but an inkling
of the coming storm, so the actor's body reacts all
the time to what is passing in his mind.   But as
passions have thoughts behind them, and every
reaction has its limitations, an actor, during the stress
of emotion as well as when calm or ecstatic, must
always remain a thinking human being (immer
Mensch bleiben). . . . His acting must always be
music. . . . He must become neither a restrained God
from Olympus nor a mere beast who surrenders
himself to his instincts. . . . He must know the
limits of the scale of his instrument. . . . He must
have a light and sensitive touch for every stage of
transition from *piano* to *forte*. . . . His words and
movements must appear from the front as if coming
instinctively in harmonious accord."

Dancing as an exercise for the actor's body is only of use if the actor can distinguish what is genuine from what are merely traditional dancers' mannerisms, which are very easily acquired and transferred on the stage, and which make an actor's movements conventional, stiff, deliberate and untrue. The majority of dancers merely watch themselves making movements and do not feel what they are doing. The so-called classes of " poses plastiques " and of " deportment " should have been abolished long ago, as they " tie up " the poor students of Dramatic Schools even more than bad dancing. " Lessons in deportment "—said Sarah Bernhardt—" have been done away with (at the Conservatoire of Paris), and rightly too. The gesture must express the thought. It will be harmonious or stupid according to the actor's intelligence. An actress moves according to the character she is playing; women who are too tall take long strides ; fat women waddle like ducks ; the arch-backed walk in Oriental fashion ; the short-legged go pitter-patter and the little ones hop. Nothing is done artificially." Sarah also remarked that long arms are a necessity on the stage and that " too long are better than too short," because " an actor with short arms can never make fine gestures." She had very long arms herself ! I usually advise my students to do healthy gymnastic exercises, to play games, and study pictures and sculpture, but never to employ gestures and poses mechanically. An actor should find *why* a certain gesture was made or why the position of a body was so executed by the artist, and then try to *imagine* those gestures and positions as his own.

As regards the study of facial expressions (so called " mimique ") which is recommended by some people, I venture to say that it only encourages the student to make meaningless grimaces. The root-cause of a facial expression is hidden deeply in our subconsciousness. To assume an expression which is to be convincingly cheerful or the contrary one must be in the mood for it. Apart from certain illustrative and imitative grimaces, all facial movements depend only on the mood of the actor.

The same applies to the study of different " tones " and " inflections." The tone in which we speak depends firstly on our feelings, and the inflection is dictated by our thoughts and feelings. The over emphasis of lines and the mimicking of the producers' inflections, so usual on the English stage, merely make the actors speech hard and feelingless, and the study of " elocution " or " declamation " leads to artificiality and mannerisms in acting. As the student of " deportment " becomes conscious of his or her movements, so the student of " elocution " becomes conscious of his voice, intonations and inflections, and that's the end of him as an actor. An actor should work at his voice and speech by studying voice production and diction, not by " elocuting."

There are several manners and " systems " of acting, in addition to the imaginative one.

K

There are actors on the stage to-day, who from fear of appearing " theatrical " try not to *act*.   They think that to seem sincere and simple they should behave as they do in everyday life in every play in which they appear—since " no one can be natural unless *he is himself*."   They exploit their own type, their mannerisms, and their particular form of attractiveness in every part they play and are in fact little more than perambulating mannequins, who are quite content to speak the playwright's words without expressing their spirit.   The majority of these " un-theatrical " actors, however, cannot resist making use of theatrical tricks in order to mask their inability to *act* with simplicity and sincerity.   I knew one actor who always ranted when rehearsing emotional scenes, but restrained himself by a trick of looking at his finger nails.   He wanted to force himself to stop thinking of the *woras* he was saying, which were making him " declaim," so he tried to concentrate while speaking on something that had nothing whatever to do with the words.   This practice resulted in his speech sounding hollow (and meaningless, too), but with this hollowness he simulated simplicity and " naturalness."   If, instead of looking at his finger nails, he had thought not of the actual words but of their *meaning*, and had used his imagination, he could have said them both simply and convincingly without any tricks.   Another actor, when acting emotional scenes, was in the habit of scratching the back of his trousers in order to make his " passionate " tirades appear "natural." Everyone knows the tricks which are used by such modern "naturalists"— they are almost a tradition. For example—to mumble monotonously, to "throw away" lines, to avoid gestures and what is called "strong acting," to talk while lighting a cigarette, to dig the toe of the shoe into the floor and keep the eyes fixed upon it (specially recommended for an actress in the part of a shy girl !), to thrust the finger nails of one hand into the palm of the other (suffering !) or to speak while chewing, etc.

Modern "naturalistic" acting is to a great extent responsible for the fact that the majority of young actors and actresses to-day suffer from atrophied imagination and neither know how to speak nor to move on the stage.

There is another manner of acting which represents a degenerate form of the romantic or "Shakespearean" school of acting, and the actors who adopt this manner, like the modern "naturalists," do not work with the imagination, but contrary to the modern "naturalists" they think it necessary to *act* on the stage. They do not make any attempt to feel or think as the characters they are playing are supposed to do. Instead of regarding their speech, movements, make up, etc., as the out-ward expression of thoughts and feelings, they *simulate*, assume different voices, intonations, inflec-tions, gestures and grimaces.

Such actors—let us call them "stagey" actors— *start* working on a part at what should be its final stage, *i.e.*, the outer expressions. Working up a part in this way usually consists of evolving and producing " rubber stamps " and effective tricks which are of about as much value as those employed by the modern naturalistic actor only of a different kind. The majority of these stamps and tricks are borrowed from what is known as the good old tradition, which abounds in clichés now used by hundreds of these stagey actors. The clichés were probably invented by some good old romantic actors as far back as the Keans, Poppe, Salbach, Charlotte Wolter, Mochalov, etc. The stagey actor utilises all this theatrical junk and serves it up to the public through the medium of his temperament, such as it is, in any and every part in any play.

The main difference between the imaginative and the stagey actor is that the former builds up his part and acts it from the " inside " while the latter watches himself from the outside producing different expressions. He makes faces, movements, inflections, because he thinks they are effective in expressing, say, grief, suffering, surprise, fear, etc. He usually invents his stage grimaces and movements before a mirror, remembers them and assumes them *without feeling the right desire* to produce them. When studying the part, he tries to speak the lines aloud with various intonations and inflections and then assumes those which he thinks are the most effective without feeling them as his own. Acting to him, is nothing but deliberate simulation; he considers the best way to make an effective " exit " or how to get a

" round " from the public ; he can wait deliberately
to " get the laughs," which would be impossible if
he were an imaginative actor, because the current of
" images " in his mind prompting his actions, could
not be disconnected without his momentarily losing
the character. A great actor like Lucien Guitry,
however, well knew how to make an " exit " or to
get a " round," but he was too great an artist not
to know how to fit that " effect " into the behaviour
of the character and how to make himself *feel* that
effect as being one of the real actions of the character,
and not just an assumed " trick."

A stagey actor can analyse what he is doing during
a performance, whereas an imaginative one puts
himself into the power of the uninterrupted sequence
of images he has created beforehand. When the
latter is supposed to hear a noise behind a door, he
actually hears it in his mind and does not simulate,
as the stagey actor would, the *effect* of having heard
it. Before taking an object from a table, he sees the
object or imagines one if there is nothing on the table.
Other images in his mind connected with that object
make him desire to take it or not to take it, or perhaps
remind him of something else associated with it,
which prompt him to perform some other action.
Before saying, for instance, " I love you," he looks
at or imagines the object of his love, and that arouses
in him the feelings contained in that line and gives
him the desire to say it. During a conversation with
a partner he looks at him and registers his every move-

ment and word, which react on him. He makes
a certain gesture or changes his position on the stage
because he feels the desire to do so, and not because
he thinks that such a movement or " cross " would
be effective.

" I analyse my part," said the French actor and
producer, Firmin Gémier, " when I am not on the
stage. If, when acting, I were to adopt certain
inflections and poses deliberately, I should become
hateful to my audience. My only desire on the stage
is to become identified with my ' character.' My
strong sensibility helps me to do that. I excel when
I feel highly strung or when a friend whose judgment
I value is in the auditorium. I am inspired by
the sympathy of the public, but probably more by
their indifference. . . . When I excel, I *live* every
situation and am no longer myself . . . the lines I
speak and the feelings of the character seems to be
me and not to have come out of the author's ink-pot."

Sometimes on the modern stage one meets actors
who attempt to combine " stagey " acting with
" imaginative " acting and others who try to com-
promise between the " stagey " and " naturalistic "
manners, but the result of these compromises and
combinations is usually disastrous.

Everyone interested in the Theatre has heard of the
system of acting expounded by Stanislavsky. The
great Russian producer, himself a fine actor, says that
the only way in which an actor can be " natural "
and sincere is to revive within himself emotional

experiences of his actual life and repeat them on the stage. He advises the actor " to discover beneath the lines of a play " what feelings prompted the author to write them, and then to recall his own feelings in similar circumstances and substitute them for those of the author.

This system of " psychic naturalism," as Stanislavsky calls it, discovered by him when working on Chehov's plays, is by no means new. Certain French theorists of the " classic " Theatre founded their systems of acting on the same outlook.

Chehov's plays were written in an entirely different manner from anything which the Moscow Art Theatre, with its naturalistic Meininger methods, had so far produced. They lacked action as understood by the old dramatists and had no obviously effective theatrical situations. " The significance of a human being and his life-drama are within him "—was a saying of Chehov. In all his plays we are shown a more or less schematic picture of life, which is drawn merely to express certain emotions and their rhythm. Chehov's characters never utter any " beautiful " speeches, which are theatrically " actable." At the vital moments they are very often silent, they repeat themselves and talk quite a lot of trivialities. It is easy to turn Chehov's plays into skits by accentuating certain points, and thus make the most tragic " inner " situation humourous.

I may. as well remark here that a Russian friend and myself rarely laughed so heartily as on seeing a

production of the " Sea Gull " in London, when the
nonsense to which this simple play had been reduced
by a " meaningful," monotonous and dreary production was accepted by the audience as a " highbrow "
affair. The " Sea Gull " seemed no less incomprehensible, when first produced by the late E. Karpov
(a very good producer of the old school) at the
St. Petersburg Imperial Alexandra Theatre and
interpreted as a drama of outer conflicts, than when
I saw it in London. It was played on that occasion
by first rate " tèrre à tèrre " actors of the realistic
school, and in spite of the acting of a couple of
artistes who were able to understand the play (amongst
whom was my sister), the " Sea Gull " at the Alexandra
Theatre was a failure. Booing and laughing started
as early as the first act. Chehov was so depressed
that he left the theatre at the fall of the curtain and
was discovered later in the night on the railway track
walking in the direction of Moscow !

Although Chehov always said that he did not know
how things should be done on the stage, he made
quite clear by his brief remarks during rehearsals of
the " Sea Gull " at the Alexandra Theatre what actors
should *not* do when acting his plays. " They're acting
too much,"—he would say. " I wish they would act
less. . . . Why walk in such an obvious way ? . . .
That fellow doesn't look a bit like a novelist. He's
simply a ' leading actor,' not a novelist ! . . . Masha
is over acting ; my Masha is simplicity itself. . . .
Everything must be done as artlessly as possible. . . .

VERA KOMISARJEVSKY IN "SISTER BEATRICE"

She plays Nina as if she had been in my soul and listened there to my intonations. . . ." A few years later, just before his death, Chehov wrote : " I still see Vera Komisarjevsky before me as Nina, and I shall never forget her in that part. . . . No one understood me so truly and deeply, as Vera Fyodorovna. . . . What a fine, sensitive actress ! . . . What a fresh, vital voice ! . . . What tones ! "

Stanislavsky recalling the experience at the Alexandra Theatre with the production of " The Sea Gull " came to the conclusion after studying the script of the play that what mattered most in " The Sea Gull " from the actors' and producer's point of view was not the story and the situations and not even the lines, but the feelings beneath the lines and their rhythmical movement. He found that Chehov intentionally *concealed* the feelings of the characters in the words they were saying and that the silences and pauses were often of much greater importance for the expression of the characters' inner life than any of their speeches. He found, too, that the inner life of Chehov's characters is intimately connected with the life of things and different sounds around them, and that these things and sounds must be made to " live " on the stage in harmony with the feelings of the players. When later he rehearsed the " Sea Gull " at the Moscow Art Theatre he made the actors start by trying to discover what the characters really thought and felt. He tried to make them live that inner life of Chehov's people as if it were their own, and to express it while speaking or in silence without the obvious actions of outer conflicts and situations employed by the old Theatre. By working a long time with the actors and helping them with the details of the production, he succeeded in realising a performance of great simplicity, sincerity and depth— what is called in German " Stimmung "—a " symphony of feelings," the realization of Maeterlinck's dream of presenting the tragedies of people's souls on the stage by means of silences and " inaction." Although the visual side of Stanislavsky's production was still devised in the old naturalistic manner of the " Meininger," the acting in this play was quite different from that in the preceding Moscow Art Theatre productions. Stanislavsky found that an actor must act " from within " and that the ensemble on the stage should be based on the " inner contacts " between the actors. When Stanislavsky tried later to " systematise " and to analyse what he had discovered intuitively, he misinterpreted himself. The idea of Stanislavsky's system can be expressed in one sentence which I once heard from his own lips, when he came to my Theatre to persuade me to become a producer at his own : " The people who breathe the air of Miasnitzkaya (a busy street in Moscow) cannot express sincerely any feelings other than those of Miasnitzkaya, and those are the feelings they must revive on the stage in order to be natural." I looked at the dear " old man " (" Starik," as everybody used to call Stanis-

lavsky in his theatre) at his enormous figure, the
high forehead with the white hair brushed back, his
penetrating but naïve eyes with the thick eye-
brows, his childish mouth and obstinate chin, and
I thought that his reasoning must always be at
odds with his intuition, which was that of a great
artist.

Speaking in his "System" about the *reproduction*
of "feelings experienced in the past," Stanislavsky
forgets that pure recollections of feelings are emotion-
ally very weak and that even if such recollected feelings
were strong enough for the purposes of acting it would
be quite impossible for an actor to make use of them.
Strong resuscitated feelings would carry with them
the past "representations" connected with them and
would therefore almost certainly dictate actions which
would have nothing to do with the play. If I love
a woman, that emotion is inseparably connected in
my mind with the image of *that* woman, and I do not
want to make any declaration of that love to some
lady provided for me by the management whose image
would simply hinder the production of my emotion.
If the management were to go to the expense or
inconvenience of engaging the woman I loved to act
with me I should certainly be ashamed to express
my sentiments to her in public. If, by any chance,
I succeeded in being so shameless as to forget the
audience, I should certainly forget also the fact that
I was on the stage, and probably act in a manner far
from that conceived by the author, and my per-

formance would develop on lines most undesirable for everyone present.

Stanislavsky suggests that the objects by which the actor is surrounded, properties, furniture, etc., must be natural and assist him to recall the feelings experienced in his life. But much that is seen when on the stage, footlights, painted flats, etc., have nothing to do with the life of the actor outside the Theatre and must act as obstacles to his " remembered feelings."

An imaginative actor needs no naturalistic copies of the environment of his personal life to help him to act, as he is able to transform any object before him into anything he chooses to make it. That is why great actors have still been great when surrounded by rags instead of scenery, and that neither the lights of the floats nor the bad make up of the cheap actors by whom they were sometimes supported, prevented them from expressing their feelings sincerely. If it were possible for an actor to act by means of " pure remembrance," his rendering of a character in any play other than one written by himself for himself, would be a complete distortion of the work of the playwright. The feelings embodied in a character are inseparable from the form in which the character is written and could not be experienced by an actor otherwise than through that form, nor expressed by him otherwise than in a manner suitable to the form of the play. Shakespeare cannot be acted in the same way as Schiller, neither of these in the same way as Shaw, nor can Shaw be acted as is Synge, nor Synge

as is Ibsen or Strindberg, and so on.   Stanislavsky
himself found the emotional movement of the " Sea
Gull," only because he understood the *form* in which
the play was written by Chehov.   Chehov's imagination, which he expressed by his peculiar manner of
writing, stimulated the imagination of Stanislavsky,
which, in its turn, acted as a stimulant on his company.
In his production of the " Sea Gull " Stanislavsky
gave an imaginative interpretation of the intentions
of Chehov.   He evolved for his company a manner
of acting which he felt to be suitable for the form
and style of the play.   The personal life of his actors
and their pure resuscitated feelings had only as much
to do with their acting as far as that personal life and
those feelings experienced in the past effected the
creative work of their imaginations.   They were
sincere in their acting because their process of creative
assimilation identified them with the characters of
Chehov, but not because they tried to be " natural "
or substituted weak emotions borrowed from their
own life for those demanded by the form of the play.

     To a producer who wanted to have everything
" natural " on the stage Chehov said : " A real nose
stuck through a portrait instead of the painted one
would be natural enough."   But the trouble is that
the nose wouldn't match the portrait and the latter
would not match the nose !   Nothing on the stage
can be called " natural," because the Theatre is a
form of art, and is therefore inventive.   Some things
frequently appear natural on the stage when the form

in which they are presented by the artist makes them appear so. I venture to think that the more " natural " the stage becomes, the more unnatural and even grotesque it will appear to everybody who sees real life as it actually is. The truth in the Theatre is always absolute in the sensation and relative in the execution. A seventeenth century French critic wrote in the " Entretiens Galants " :—" Le récit des comédiens dans le tragique est une manière *de chant*, et la Champmeslé donne des infléxions si *naturelles* qu'il semble qu'elle ait véritablement dans le cœur une passion. . . ." Champmeslé, the famous French actress who played in Racine's tragedies, used a formal, unnatural style of acting, singing and making " plastic " gestures to suit the style of Racine, yet her talent made her audiences believe in her acting as in an invented truth. By calling her inflections "natural," the critic really meant " sincere" and "convincing." Apart from the fact that acting is a creative art and not mimicry, and that every play—a work of a creative mind—must be acted in a way suitable to its form and style, an actor must take into consideration the size of the stage and the dimensions and the acoustics of the auditorium. He must know not only how to transpose—to use the musical expression—his tone and actions from the "life key" to the "key of the play" but also how to adapt his expressions to the frame and to the space in which he has to act, and what would appear unnatural in life, seems the truth itself when done by a good actor and seen from the auditorium.

CHAPTER SIX

The " synthetic " Theatre and the " universal " actor—Dynamic décors—The " baroque " stage—My productions of Opera abroad—My work in " commercial " Theatres—" Highbrow " Theatre in England—Experiments in Paris—The producer's business—My methods of rehearsing and producing—The Cinema v. Theatre—The amateurs

WHEN producing my first musical piece, " The Queen of May," in 1908 and prior to that when watching operatic performances, I came to the conclusion that opera, because it can combine all the expressions of the actor's art—movement, speech, singing—could be the most perfect form of Theatrical art, and have the most powerful appeal to the public. This would be true, too, of a representation of a play in which all the various branches of the actor's art were *synthetically* united. An actor who played in such a synthetic show would have to possess a knowledge and practice of music, poetry, singing and dancing, and would have to be master of every means of theatrical expression and, therefore, a perfect performer, a *universal* actor, as I call him. After all, a perfect actor of the drama, even if he is not required to sing, must also be a universal actor. He must be able to combine all the forms of expression he has to use, create a synthesis of them subordinating all of them

143

to his conception of the part and to the single rhythm*
of his emotions.   Without an understanding and
practice of rhythm an actor cannot feel the text
of the playwright and cannot achieve the necessary
symmetry of the emotional movement in his mind
with the movement of his speech and his body.   Only
rhythmical speech and movement is expressive of the
creative mind.

From the point of view of acting the only difference
between the opera and the drama is that whereas in
the former the melody of speech is notated, in the
latter it remains under-developed, and has to be found
by the actor in his lines.   Both the drama and the
opera in their present state are deficient as forms of
Theatrical art.   In opera, the purely musical and vocal
side prevails, and the singers neglect the art of acting
and of speaking, whereas in drama actors have no
feeling for the rhythm and the music of speech.   In
neither the one nor the other do the players understand
that their bodies must be trained to be responsive
instruments to the rhythmic impulses of the score or
of the play.   The ballet is also deficient as a form of
Theatrical art.   The dancers, with very few exceptions, cannot act and may be compared to posing
acrobatic automata, some with more calories of temperament, some with less, some without any at all.

This division of the art of the Theatre into drama,

------

* The Russian poet Andrey Byely defines rhythm as " the
singing of the soul " and Jacques Dalcroze as " the symmetry
of movement and accent."

opera and ballet is purely artificial and enforced, and perfection in Theatrical art can be achieved only by a synthetic union of the drama, opera and ballet in one single show, in which each of these would be the complement of the other, which would be performed by an ensemble of universal actors.

The fact that the actors of to-day have very little idea of how to harmonize emotion, voice, movement and their surroundings, is one of the main reasons why it is so difficult on the modern stage to achieve unity, an ensemble and to create an " atmosphere " in any production. If the actors possessed more sensitive eyes and ears, and understood something about the art of composition of bodies, of lines and colours, and studied their bodily movements through the medium of music they would soon realise how disconnected, and even antagonistic, speech and movement are in their own performances, and how very often they don't " fit " into the sounding dynamic pictures of which they should be a part.

If the modern dramatic actor is deficient as an artist of the Theatre, the operatic singer of our time is even worse. His performance is little more than a recital in fancy dress, accompanied by totally un-necessary, often fatuous, and unmusical gestures, which have the most irritating effect on a sensitive spectator. An operatic performer of to-day never acts *because* of and *with* the music, and never interprets its rhythm in his movements. He merely produces mechanically certain stock movements and gestures,

L

thinks only of his voice, the notes he is singing, and of keeping tune.

But he is not alone to blame, since the operas themselves very seldom give him scope for real musical acting. No one can act " unactable " material consisting of a series of solos and ensembles, written merely for singing purposes and artificially strung together. Even Wagner, although he insisted that the actors' movements should be dictated by the music, does not give his interpreters enough opportunity for acting. In the first place, the vocal difficulties which his parts present are very often such that the artistes are constrained to forget everything beyond the question of producing their voices. Secondly, the Wagnerian love of interminable static " monologues " and duets (as for instance, Tristan's musical speech at the beginning of the last scene of the opera, and the Love Duet in the garden) lack movement and thus give no scope for acting. Thirdly, although Wagner called his operas " musical dramas," very few (except perhaps " Die Meistersinger ") are *theatrical* musical dramas. Everything Wagner wished to express in his operas he expressed fully through the medium of the orchestral music itself, using the singers' voices as parts of the orchestra score. The " illustration " of the music by the movements of the singers, as required in Wagner's books, is not only superfluous, but takes his music out of the infinite region of time and drags it down into the narrowness of three dimensional space. Furthermore,

PERMANENT SETTING FOR MOZART'S "COSI FAN TUTTE." Teatro di Torino, 1927. Komisarjevsky. An Italian critic wrote about this production: "Raramente c'ero Stato possibile gustare la Musica di un' opera di Mozart [e dico Mozart come potrei dire qualunque altro grande operista] e guardare contemporaneamente la scena. Komisarjevsky ha fatto questo miracolo."

neither the bodily size of the actors nor the emotions of ordinary human beings, nor sets—not even those of Appia—could satisfy the imagination of those who understand and love the music of Wagner's " musical dramas."

An opera in which pure music predominates should be performed not in a Theatre but statically like an oratorio in a concert hall. The music of a " musical play " must be dynamic, to act with, and to express the moods of the characters, the rhythm, the tempi, the crescendi, the diminuendi, and every point and accent of the action. An ideal example of this is to be found for instance in the final ensemble of the first act of Mozart's " Cosi Fan Tutte " and in bits of some of the Moussorgsky operas. In a production of a musical play the music must find its expression in the acting, and the musical elements, as for instance poly-rhythm and counterpoint, must find their visible equivalents in the movements and grouping of the actors and the crowds on the stage.

To make a fully harmonious impression on the audience a Synthetic Theatre requires something entirely new in the matter of décor—something dynamic in place of what is at present static. In the realistic Theatre the sets merely serve as an indication of locality ; in the symbolic Theatre, as a " picture," expressive perhaps of the mood of *one single* moment of the performance, but not in keeping with the different moods of other moments : in the so-called

" bio-mechanical " Theatre as a static construction devised for the purposes of moving and placing the actors. The dynamic rhythm of the music expressed by the action should be reflected in the dynamic environment of the actor. The dynamic décor of the Synthetic Theatre should be in harmony with the music and the ensemble of performers. Even in a production of a play without music the rhythm of the stage action should reflect itself in the surroundings. As the action constantly *moves*, since it is subject to the different changes of mood of the play, so the surroundings cannot remain static during the performance nor react with their unchangeable colours and lines on the spectator as one single static mood. Unless the actors are performing on a " neutral," indifferent background, which does not affect the emotions of the spectators, and does not interfere with the rhythm of the action, the décor must be in dynamic harmony with the acting and should be made to change, if not always its forms— which would perhaps not be impossible in the productions of some realistic plays without destroying the atmosphere of reality—at least the colours and effects of light and shade. Everybody knows that with certain combinations of colour and lines just as with combinations of sounds and movements, one can achieve a definite psychic effect on the spectator. Nobody can get as complete an impression from a theatrical performance as from a " single " work of art while listening simultaneously to poetry and music and at the same time looking at the " décors " and watching people move or dance, unless all these different forms are brought into inner harmony with each other. In the modern Theatre we get a discord of different forms of artistic expression in every show, and strangely enough nobody on the stage notices it. But every sensitive spectator has to make an effort to forget the scenery in order to watch the acting and listen to the music and the rest of the production. Very often, in order to concentrate on the meaning of the actor's words he has to shut his eyes to avoid seeing his movements, and in order to watch his movements, he has to stop up his ears so as not to hear the lines.

All the arts utilised on the stage of a Synthetic Theatre should convey simultaneously the same feelings and ideas to the spectator. The rhythm of the music must be in harmony with the rhythm of the words, with the rhythm of the movements of the actors, of the colours and lines of the décors and costumes, and of the changing lights. The reaction on the spectator of musical acting must be strengthened by this synthetic environment.

I put these ideas on the Synthetic Theatre into practice for the most part in my own Theatres in Russia. In my Moscow School with the assistance of my great friend, Valdemar Bernardi, who was my musical director, and is one of the finest *theatrical* musicians I have ever met—nowadays one of the many exiles in Paris—I trained my students to be " universal " actors. Quite a number of them to my great satisfaction are at the present moment both good singers and good actors and have good jobs.

Experimenting with my dynamic décors I found that lighting afforded the best means by which to realize my ideas and that, until the seventeenth century "baroque" stage and auditorium, still used in modern theatres are abolished, the best possible "décor" is a high plain screen or wall at the back and sides of the stage and a floor, the levels of which can be changed. The "baroque" peep-show box stage intended for static décors painted in perspective, for three wall interiors and for the old-fashioned division of plays into "acts" is an anachronism. The quick, impatient modern mind with its syncopated, jumping rhythm is bored by the old "expositions," "developments" and "conclusions" of situations, by the gradual leading up to the climaxes and by the intervals between the artificially concocted acts of the quasi-modern plays. We need quick action in the Theatre without any intervals occupied by the present antediluvian way of shifting scenery and "props." We no longer want the Aristotelian or Ibsenian regular "acts" or "scenes." We need, sometimes, in the midst of a scene a flash into the past or the future. We need different actions happening simultaneously in various places on the stage—on the right, on the left, somewhere high above—accompaniments of "expressionistic" noises, and of moving lights from the front, the back, the sides, above and

"The Tales of Hoffman." The Doll Scene. Moscow, 1919. Komisarjevsky.

below the actors, an orchestra which would not sit between the spectators and the stage with a " star " conductor waving his baton and trying by every conceivable means to be conspicuous to the public. We don't want any old fashioned " class " divisions of auditoriums into stalls, pits and galleries. We need comfortable seats for every individual of the public from each of which the whole stage would be visible. In brief, we need new Theatrical buildings which would not resemble the existing baroque " show-houses " at all. Before I came to this conclusion I employed *moving* sets, *transparent* sets, changing colours and varying intensities of lights, gauzes in front of the stage to diffuse and reflect the lights, etc., but have always been handicapped by the deficient equipment of Theatres.

The above-mentioned productions of my Moscow Theatre last season, my productions of " Lohengrin," Beethoven's " Fidelio " and Rossini's " Barbiere " at the Soviet Opera House, as well as those of " Parsifal " and Mozart's " Don Giovanni " for the Imperial Theatre, as far as circumstances allowed me, were conceived on the lines of the Synthetic Theatre. Since leaving Russia I have had very little chance of putting my ideas on the Synthetic Theatre into practice and have seldom been able to work in the ordinary operatic or dramatic Theatres in the way I wanted and used to in Russia.

I was not able to do much, when, for instance, I was given an opera, to produce in one of the "famous Opera Houses in the World," in three days—and that, too, with a company quite unacquainted with the music, with old and incomplete sets which I never saw until the actual performance, and which had to be patched up just before the curtain rose. On the first night of another of my productions at the same Opera House, one of Wagner's operas, which was rehearsed and produced in two and a half days' time, I had to prompt nearly every movement to the chorus and to some of the soloists from the wings. Of course they never coincided with the music as demanded by the score, and the general confusion and bewilderment on the stage at certain moments was such that I thought we should have to lower the curtain, but to my great astonishment the management after the end of the performance was "delighted with the success." When I produced "Siegfried" at another Theatre, and in another country, a star tenor, either a German or Dutchman, refused to sing his part a few minutes before the curtain went up unless I agreed to put an enormous boarding-house sofa on the stage among my set of "stylised" rocks, jumping on which would enable him to give an exhibition of the youthful temperament of Siegfried. But that was not all. During the two rehearsals which he deigned to attend—since, as a "star" he took the liberty of staying away from the others—he refused point-blank to take up the positions which I indicated, saying that he had sung the part hundreds of times and that in his own opinion his interpretation could not be improved upon, since it was exactly the same as that of all the great Wagnerian singers, and that, anyway, he was past the stage in which he could learn anything from anybody. Once I had to deal with a prima-donna who did not come to any of the rehearsals, another time with a conductor who let his assistant conduct all the rehearsals, appeared only before the curtain went up and was very indignant that I had made the chorus act and move, mixing all the voices up and not having them in the " traditional " way—the sopranos and tenors standing on the O.P. side and the altos and basses on the P. side or *vice versa*. By the way, operatic conductors who are interested in the *production* of an opera, are very rare, and as the majority of the operas to be acted and produced have to be rearranged, cut and dealt freely with, the average operatic conductor is usually the worst enemy of a producer. I even met one (an excellent concert conductor) who was jealous not only of the success of the producer but of the successes of the singers ; he tried by all possible means to put into prominence the work of his orchestra, this very often nullifying the efforts of everybody on the stage, and even drowned the voices of the singers when he thought them dangerous for his personal success. Since 1919 I have produced in England, France and Italy sixteen Operas and only two of these operas have I been able to produce without being overwhelmed by obstacles such as I have described and even those two had to

be done in a very short time. The first was " Cosi
Fan Tutte " at the Teatro di Torino at Turin, and
the second Moussorgsky's " The Fair of Sorotchin,"
which I did for the Opera Privé in Paris, a new venture
of the famous Russian singer, Mme. Kouznetzov-
Massenet.

In the " commercial " dramatic Theatres I have
often had " leading " actors in my castes who even
if they behaved charmingly and did not dictate their
wishes to me as openly as the famous Dutch or
German singer did, usually took unwarranted liberties
with the plays, adapting them to their " personalities "
in order to satisfy their egotism and vanity.   I had to
make quite illegitimate concessions to them in order
to make it possible to produce a play at all.   As
selfishness on the stage is a contagious disease, everyone else in the company began to behave in the same
way as the stars, and whole shows merely degenerated
into a series of Variety turns by different performers,
each on his own.   In one production an actress
playing the part of a plain, shabbily dressed country
girl, definitely refused, albeit with a sweet smile, to
appear on the stage without a " pretty " frock, and
came on on the first night dressed like an operatic
soubrette with her face made up like a doll.   When
I remarked that her appearance gave a wrong impression of the character and ruined the idea of the
play, she answered that " the public would hate to
see her in rags."   In another production I could not
restrain an actor-manager, who had to represent an

old, modest and unhappy middle class man, from behaving like a King in melodrama. I was even blamed in several papers for a great deal of the " business " forced upon me by that actor-manager, who did not object at all to it not being in keeping with the character he had to represent, nor even to being quite absurd from the point of view of the story of the play, so long as it got him " the sympathy of the audience." On one occasion I was obliged to give a big part to a relation of the " backer " of the play, a young lady, who had not the slightest idea of acting, and who interfered with all my directions, not only those affecting her own part but everyone else's as well. She interrupted my work at the most trying moments of rehearsal by teaching me how to produce, walking about and holding loud conversations in the corners of the rehearsal room and did her best, as I told her in exasperation, to turn the place into " a Turkish bazaar."

In what is despisingly called the " highbrow " Theatre in England, a producer is always handicapped by an almost total lack of money. He can neither engage the actors he wants, nor have a sufficient number of rehearsals, and his resources from the scenic point of view are of the most meagre description. I did some very interesting productions on a small and economical scale—for the " Stage Society " (" The Race with the Shadow " by Wilhelm von Scholz, " Uncle Vanya," K. Hamsun's " At the Gates of the Kingdom," Pirandello's " Six Characters in

Search of an Author " in 1921–22, and Arnold
Bennett's " The Bright Island " in 1925); at some of
the small suburban Theatres (The Everyman and the
Barnes Theatre); and under my own management
(" Paul the First " by Merejkovsky and A. Bennett's
" Mr. Prohack " at the Court Theatre, and my own
play, " The Brass Paperweight," written on the theme
of Dostoyevsky's " Karamazov's " at the Apollo
Theatre), but always with the greatest difficulties.
Although everyone who played in these productions
of mine—amongst whom were many good London
actors (Leon Quartermaine, Franklyn Dyall, Leslie
Banks, George Hayes, Michael Sherbrooke, George
Relph, Cathleen Nesbitt, Isabel Jeans, Lydia Sherwood,
Dorothy Green and others) with whom I enjoyed
working—was always keen on being produced by me,
it hardly ever happened that the whole caste was
present at a single rehearsal.   I could not, of course,
blame anybody, as the artistic managements had not
the means with which to pay the actors adequately,
and they were obliged to think first of their jobs in the
commercial theatre in order to live, and could give
the " highbrow " experiments only their spare time.
In these productions I very seldom held a rehearsal on
a stage.   They usually took place in some tiny, dingy
room without the necessary furniture and props, and
I was never able to see the whole scene of the action
or to guess how the play would sound on the stage.
I very seldom had a rehearsal with the sets before the
one and only dress rehearsal and quite often had to

TROTSKY, LENIN AND TROTSKY'S WIFE IN A SCENE FROM "RED SUNDAY,"
a play by by Hubert Griffith produced by Komisarjevsky in London (1929).
This play was done for four special performances but was not allowed
to be put on for an ordinary run.

arrange the lighting during the intervals of the actual performance. In my " Stage Society " productions I was obliged to use one convertible set, designed by myself, for every production, and had to make ten different interiors and exteriors out of it. This was more or less the case when I had to produce in the little " highbrow " Theatres or under my own " poor " management. The managers of the little London Theatres asked me to make settings costing next to nothing, saying that I was " so clever at doing things cheaply and yet making them seem expensive and just the right thing." I am sure I was. Once, for financial reasons, we had to make the sets for the production of Andreyev's " Katerina " at Barnes in the Theatre itself, without even a workshop, and as the carpenter, who happened to be the electrician and the property master at the same time, confessed after a week's effort that he could not manage it, my stage manager and friend, Mr. Keith Moss (a real master of all trades), and myself had to finish the work for him. The result was that we had no sets for the dress rehearsal and that nothing was finished for the actual performance. The curtain went up on the first night of our " artistic " show forty minutes late! During the intervals I had to improvise the sets, because some of the flats, backings, etc., were missing, others were dripping wet, or had ceilings which did not fit, etc. As Keith Moss had collapsed from exhaustion and had been taken home half unconscious just before the show, I had to set the stage and do the prompting myself.   On another occasion when I had no experienced stage manager at all and was unable to have the scenery (for Chehov's "Ivanov" at the same Theatre) before the actual night of the show, the set collapsed while the carpenters were putting it up during an interval, and if I had not been standing by the curtain and had not had the strength to hold a couple of flats on my head and in my hands, they would have fallen into the auditorium and might have killed a couple of the spectators.

I enjoyed my work at the Théâtre des Champs Elysées in Paris where I produced plays under the management of Jacques Hébertot in 1923–24. Hébertot who is a tall, very delightful and enterprising man with interesting modern ideas, lost a large amount of money on propaganda for the "avant garde" Theatre, but he helped to "launch" the modern Parisian producers, Gaston Baty, Jouvet and Pitoeff, all of whom are doing very well now.   But there too, I was handicapped by lack of money to spend on actors' salaries, scenery and costumes, as were all the other producers.   Still, we worked like oxen, often not leaving the Theatre until the early hours of the morning, and with the encouragement from our "patron" Hébertot we succeeded in achieving, perhaps poor and unfinished, but new and interesting productions.   I remember that after the first night of my production of a Chinese play, written by Henri Duvérnois and Pascal Fortuny, "Le Club des

Costume for the Duenna. Sheridan's " The Duenna," produced in 1923 at the " Comédie des Champs Elysées," Paris. Komisarjevsky.

Canards Mandarins," I read at the Café "Chèz Francis," where we all used to go, Antoine's criticism in the paper, in which he called me, " Un régisseur qui par ce premier essai chèz nous se revèle maître," which of course gave me great pleasure.

On another occasion when I produced " The Dover Road " by A. A. Milne in English in Paris, the managers ran away because they had no money to pay for the production ! A similar thing happened when I started a small " Arc-en-Ciel " Theatre in Paris in 1925. Just before the dress rehearsal I discovered that my co-operators, who had led me to believe that they had quite a lot of money, could not pay the bills and that the manager had run away. The dressmaker who had been engaged to make the costumes (an old lady who had never made any theatrical dresses before, but had been given the order because she was cheap) refused to bring the costumes to the Theatre until she was paid. When at last twenty-four hours before the first performance the costumes arrived they were unfinished and in such a state, that I had to beg some volunteers—friendly ladies—to come to the Theatre and sit all night sewing, trying to make those costumes look like costumes, and all for a cup of tea and some sandwiches. When the public started to arrive for the show, the artist who had decorated the auditorium and had not been paid, arrived in a fury and started to tear some plaster ornaments he had designed off the walls. He was followed by the chief carpenter

with a hammer who threatened to smash all the
mirrors in the lounge if he were not paid on the spot,
and I had to use the utmost strategy to get them out
of the auditorium into the office.

I could say much more about the " fun " I have had
out of my " artistic " ventures since 1919, but it would
require a special volume. With time, however, I got
accustomed to working under such stimulating circumstances and came to look upon them as part of a new
experience—a struggle to achieve something almost
impossible. Still such conditions were often very
cramping and prevented me from being able to work
in the way I should have liked to.

I always thought that it is the ensemble of the actors
which makes a Theatre and not the producer, and that
in order for the latter to do his work properly, not
considering the actors as mere clay in his hands, there
must be a mutual sympathetic understanding between
the actors and the producer, the latter not being
regarded as a drilling-sergeant. This understanding
cannot be acquired at once. The producer must know
his actors, to be able to inspire and direct them and not
look upon them as so many moving and talking
automata for the purpose of carrying out his orders.
A theatrical producer's work is more or less the same
as that of a symphony orchestra conductor. The main
difference between conductor and producer is that the
work of the former is seen by the public, and he is
able to inspire and control the orchestra during the
performance, while that of the latter is not seen by

the audience, and he is powerless during the performance. Of course, a producer must have a knowledge of many more things than an ordinary conductor in order to be able to produce plays efficiently. He must have a sound understanding of all the arts which are always involved in the Theatre—literature, sculpture, painting, architecture and music. He must not only know the so-called " technique of acting," but also possess a fine sense of psychology, because the " inside " of an actor—call it " soul," " consciousness," or whatever you like —with which the producer has to deal, is a very complicated and delicate instrument. That instrument is what matters most on the stage and only an extremely sensitive and careful producer can play on it without hurting the freshness of the actor's conception of the part and his own creation of it. Of course, what I am telling now about a theatrical producer only concerns the Theatre of art, where plays have some inner meaning to them which is to be interpreted scenically. The commercial Theatre needs no producing nor does the Theatre of the " stars." Those who, in that Theatre, show the actors where to come from and where to go to, how to serve up to the public some borrowed stock effects or how to stimulate inflections and gestures, are not producers in the sense in which I use the word. They are merely experts at " stage business " in addition to " box office business."

When working in Russia I usually started my

M

rehearsals by gathering the company round a table or round a piano and had several readings of the play or singings of the opera and talks about them. I considered such " sitting " or " standing " rehearsals just as important as the " walking " ones. I never read plays to the actor myself for fear that they might get into the way of imitating my reading of it. I then talked to them about the play and gave them my conception of the production and how I imagined the characters and their surroundings and produced sketches of the sets and costumes. Before the first of these talks every actor received a script of the whole play (not a " part ") or the full score, if a musical production. After the reading of the play and the first talk, the company had a day or two off in which to make closer acquaintance with the play and their parts, and then the sitting rehearsals were resumed. I never forced my actors, before all else, to learn their lines. On the contrary, I advised them not to do so, as such parrot-like learning kills that spontaneity of feeling which is essential in order to speak lines sincerely. An author's words, learned mechanically, never can become, as they should do, an actor's own. During the sitting rehearsals the company repeated the lines after the prompter (we had a special prompter in Russia), concentrating their attention particularly on the motive of the lines, as well as on their meaning. Careful attention was paid to the action and to all the stages of transition or emotion and thought. During the sitting rehearsals

"SIEGFRIED." The Forest Scene. 1923. Komisarjevsky.

my actors got sincerity into their rendering, and both the " desire " to say the lines and perform the actions as if they were prompted by their own feelings. I observed the creative process in the actor's own minds and *directed* them in their search for the right rendering of the lines and the attendant movement. When they found it themselves I helped to perfect their methods of expression. I think a producer should know how to make expressions come to life in an actor's mind and not to force intonations, and movements upon him, which have been invented in the producer's study before rehearsals. If I have to show an actor an outer expression, inflection, gesture or movement, I always try at the same time to make his imagination work and to arouse in him the *desire* for such expression. I give him not only a picture of the situation in which he finds himself at the moment of the required expression together with the reason and the aim of that expression, but also its inner connection with the preceding moment in his acting of which the expression must be a direct result. We worked round the table until each actor had mastered his character and found the continuity of his actions and the links between himself and the other characters of the play. Having got thus far the actors themselves usually expressed the wish to rehearse on the stage and act " with movements." Knowing the motives for their own and each other's actions they were able to find roughly their positions and even their movements, these being merely the expressions of what they actually had in their minds. Those positions and movements more or less coincided with those in my producer's script, because in preparing the script I always acted the parts myself and later at the " sitting " rehearsals I watched the actors' individual ways of expressing my intentions and, if necessary, altered or adapted the original directions of my script so as to suit their individuality, at the same time not upsetting my conception of the production.

The work of a producer on a production is a matter of composition just as is any other work of art. It is like devising an animated coloured talking and moving sculpture. The preliminary home work of a producer is only the first sketch. During the sitting rehearsals, when he has the actual performers in front of him, hears voices, sees their faces and watches the creative process in their minds, he enriches and alters his conception and makes the second sketch. Only at the walking rehearsals and when seeing the play as a whole in movement in its actual setting, can the producer give his composition definite form. At that stage he brings the cast into inner as well as outer contact, establishes the rhythmical movement of the action and perfects and fixes the movements and the positions of the actors in the sets.

Working with the company is to me always the most interesting part of the job, although the least effective. A producer never gets any credit for his work with the cast. When the public praises a " production " they usually refer to the visual " spectacle," or aspect of the show. It is quite a usual thing for a critic or a spectator to think that simple plays are not *produced*, because the sets are not striking and the dresses have no colours, and because, in fact, nothing is obvious. Actually, one simple scene of a play by Shaw, Galsworthy or Chehov, to be interpreted on the stage, requires more talent on the part of the producer than all the " magnificent productions " of revues with their elaborate sets, lighting effects, and bevies of girls, dressed (or undressed !) in a most striking way. It needs much more brain and art to interpret a deep feeling at a simple, unobtrusive moment than to present sensational sets and costumes, women's bodies, horses, crowds of supers, and all the rest of the paraphernalia of a big show. The better a producer and his company are, the less obvious for the spectator is his work with single actors and with the ensemble. If it *is* noticeable it is merely a sign that either his company could not assimilate his directions or that he was unable to inspire them and make their imaginations work and merely used them as so many automata to carry out his directions. A showy producer, keen on personal success, concentrates his attention on the sets, lighting, costumes, supers and different effective " bits of business " instead of on the acting. The real producer uses no " production tricks " and devises the sets, lighting and costumes to serve the purposes required by the acting and as expressions of his idea of the production and of the inner movement of the play. From this it is clear that unless the producer can find an artist who can express his ideas, he must design the sets and the costumes and light the production himself.   A real production is in the first place psychological, and pictorial only in the second place.   The producer first gets a broad conception of the production, of its form and style.   Then he conceives—visualises and hears—each character, and then puts all of them into rythmical movement. Only then does he visualise the environment best suited for the expression of the movement, and invents the sets, their ground plans and levels, the colours and directions of his lighting, etc.   The furniture, every detail on the stage, serve the same purpose as the sets, *i.e.*, to suit the acting and not vice versa.   In constructing the sets the producer should not lose sight of the fact that the life *in* them is connected with life *around* them ; this helps to create what is called an atmosphere and to make the sets seem " alive."

Of course my methods of working with actors when producing films in Russia were very different, as the arts of the Theatre and Cinema require very different forms of expression.   I was unable however, to apply any method to my work on a film which I produced in England owing to the most primitive conditions under which it had to be made.   I was allowed only five weeks for the whole production, an absurdly inadequate time for the required work, and was given the scenario only a couple of days before the actual " shooting."   It was written so badly that it was impossible to work from it and I had eventually to improvise the whole thing while taking the shots.   I had none of the equipment required for a modern film—insufficient lighting apparatus and no facilities for any interesting shots.   The sets were not designed by me and most of them without my approval. They were built so badly that it was almost impossible to use them as backgrounds for " close-ups."   The camera-man and myself were not allowed to " waste the precious time " in finding expressive lighting or suitable angles for the shots.   It was impossible to retake any of the shots as the sets were struck before I could see any of them on the screen.   As I had to be " on the floor " from 9 a.m. until 11 p.m. every day, I was always told when I asked to see some of the work done, that the operator had gone home or that the theatre was shut etc.   It is not surprising that there is a " crisis " in the British Film Industry if some other British producers have to work under similar conditions and little wonder that the Germans and the Americans who are able to work under normal conditions produce occasionally something besides badly-made trivialities.

A good deal has been written lately about the menace to the legitimate Theatre of the talking films, but on the contrary if films continue to be produced on the lines I have described and producers do not use a new " technique " for expressing life and ideas on the screen through an exclusive medium of the camera and not through the medium of the stage, as is customary now, films, silent, coloured or talkie will become merely a " preserved " theatrical entertainment, and will destroy themselves as an independent form of art. The advent of the silent pictures did not bring about the expected " death of the Theatre " and nor will the talkies. On the contrary, the *real* Theatre will benefit because of them. Photography has not killed the art of painting nor have the gramophone and the wireless affected concerts and recitals, and despite machine-work there is still a demand for " hand-made " goods. The " talkies " are merely putting the Theatre in its right place and are bringing it's real value into prominence. It was inconceivable that in this age of machinery there would not come a " mechanical " Theatre, and the results of the perfection of this mechanisation may bring to the modern Cinema everything which it lacks at present. Probably later when the perfect combination of the wireless and television has been effected it will not be necessary to go to a " Picture Palace," one will even be able to enjoy these " mechanical performances " at one's Club during lunch or dinner. But what we will never be able to enjoy in the mechanical Theatre is the living contact with the actor. The art of acting on the screen is and will always remain a kind of " tinned " acting, transmitted to the public through a machine, the laws of which are and must be those of the art of the Cinema. The power of the stage over the public lies in the living vital acting of a real human being whose bodily and mental presence the

"Fata Malerba," Opera by Guy. The first act. Teatro di Torino, 1927. Komisarjevsky.

spectator *feels* during the performance, as the actor on the stage feels the presence of his spectators and gets inspiration from them, and it is this which makes his acting live freshly with each separate performance. The screen can supply all the paraphernalia of the spectacular side of the stage and much that is beyond the scope of the stage, but the living contact and the " soul " of an actor cannot be transmitted in the mechanical Theatre. The influence of the talking films on the Theatre will be beneficial for the latter. It will result in much bigger demands being made of the actors of the Theatre. It will eventually convince managers and producers that the strength of the stage does not lie in the " spectacles " and outer effects and tricks in productions, all of which could be done more lavishly and incomparably better by the Cinema, but in the interpretation of good plays " of the Theatre " by good actors and by the crowds. Again as the Cinema becomes an increasingly popular entertainment owing to the elaborate and expensive productions it can offer to the public at reasonable prices, the greater public will desert the Theatre in favour of the Cinema and there will be less chance for the gamblers in the Theatre.

As regards the Cinema, the magic of its art lies essentially in the possibilities of the lighting and the camera ; the latter should be exploited and not merely used as a kind of spectator for registering anæmic or complicated theatrical dramas or comedies. The camera must create and compose, as well as reproduce. It must register not only people and objects but also the symbolic and relative expressions of their inner life and meaning. In addition, the camera must not only compose but also " decompose " ob ects and people into elements, and make new compositions of such elements ; it must use " abstract " forms and give " photograms " of thoughts and feelings.

As the power of the stage over the public lies almost exclusively in acting so the power of films lies in their composition. The objects, the lighting, the distances and angles of the shots, their sequence and the rhythmical movement within each individual shot of a film, and within each sequence are of a similar value for a film as are the actors for a play. An actor is only a small element of the general composition. The less the actor " acts," the better it is for the result of the whole film, and one of the first requirements of a film actor is, that he must possess a physique which will convey the producer's intention, and often a producer will discover a type, who knows very little about acting, but is pliable material and more useful for expressing his intentions than a trained actor. The best actor for the stage however, is one who can create his characters through his imagination and who understands the synthetic ensemble of the production.

It was not until eight years after leaving Russia that I succeeded in 1927—thanks to a very good and keen company and a management consisting of people like signori Gualino, Venturi and Gatti, who are fond of

" The Tidings brought to Mary," by Paul Claudel.   The Farewell Supper Scene.   The N.Y.   Theatre   Guild,
1922.   Komisarjevsky.

the Theatre and not only of the box office —in achieving (with less than a fortnight's rehearsal) a more or less synthetic production of the aforementioned "Cosi Fan Tutte" at the Teatro di Torino in Turin with settings and costumes designed by myself. I tried to put some of my synthetic theories into practice and make use of dynamic lighting in some of my other productions, in—" The Tidings brought to Mary," in some scenes of " Peer Gynt," which I did for the Theatre Guild in New York, in " King Lear," and in " The 14th of July " by R. Rolland, when I did them (in 1927 and 1928) for the delightful and enthusiastic boys of the Oxford University Dramatic Society. But, as a rule I have neither had the necessary actors, nor the financial means, nor the time to continue working on the lines of a purely synthetic Theatre. Still, I have always had those ideas in my mind when producing a play, no matter what the circumstances may have been. The " musical " ensemble of the actors has been my aim in every one of my productions, operatic as well as dramatic. The perfection of the actor's art has always been my object. When producing I interpret a play by every artistic means the stage (and the money, of course) allows me, and try to form a harmonious synthesis. In my interpretation I try to convey to the audience not only the story and the ideas contained in the play (if there are any!) but the music and rhythm (which can be discovered in any play) which is expressive of its emotional content.

The big success of my production of " The Three
Sisters " in London at the Barnes Theatre was largely
due to the fact that I evolved the way to convey
Chehov's inner meaning and made the rhythm of the
" music " of the play blend with the rhythm of the
movements of the actors, giving the necessary accents
with the lighting and the various outer " effects."   If
this synthesis had not been completely harmonious the
play might have seemed thin and even meaningless to
the audience, as indeed, it did during rehearsals to the
majority of the actors until they observed the final result.

I have done quite a number of productions with
amateurs (besides those for the O.U.D.S.) since
leaving Russia, and I must say that they take their
work   much   more   to   heart   and   are   much   less
selfish than professionals, and the results of the work
with them are usually much more fresh and sincere.
They have a strong advantage over " actors "—the
fact of being " inexperienced " which makes it
practically impossible for them to see the Theatre
from the stagey point of view, and forces them to
use their imagination and to express themselves on the
stage not in terms of theatrical experience but from the
experience of their own lives.

One of my last works with amateurs was when
I produced Ibsen's " The Pretenders " in Welsh for
the National Festival at Holyhead at the request of
Lord Howard de Walden, whose activities are of
enormous assistance in supporting and fostering the
amateur Theatre movement in the British Isles.

Every Saturday during the Summer of 1927 Lord Howard de Walden, myself, and the stage manager, Miss G. Vernon, took the 8 a.m. train from London to Bangor to rehearse there in the afternoon. Everyone taking part in the production worked during the week as teachers, parsons, clerks, postmen, miners and so forth, and were only free to rehearse after tea on Saturdays. The play was a very difficult one and at the start it seemed to me that Lord Howard de Walden considered the whole business pretty hopeless. The " actors " got into their parts very slowly, and it was no easy job to get over the poor diction and enunciation and the monotony of phrasing and the bodily stiffness of some of the players. But as the rehearsals proceeded and I managed to make them less conscious of what they were doing and saying, and more interested in the *meaning* of what they had to say and do, they began to " feel " their parts and gradually and successfully assimilated my directions. One cannot expect amateurs, who act very seldom compared to professionals, to have any, " technique," a thing which is only acquired by actual practice on the stage. Towards the end, some of them, for instance the players acting the parts of Skule and Hakon gave very good performances indeed, compared to which, I am sorry to say, the same parts as played in the West End of London by certain professionals were weak and lifeless. I noticed that the less " experienced " my players were, *i.e.*, the less they imitated professionals, the better were their performances. The interest and

keenness of everyone in their work was quite extraordinary. I had a crowd of about 150 people composed
of inhabitants of the town, and I was often stopped in
the streets the week before the performance, while
staying at Holyhead, by a milkman pushing his cart or
a postman delivering letters in order to talk about the
rehearsals. An old gentleman acting the part of the
Bishop showed such interest in his part that during the
performance he tried to deliver a long speech which I
had decided to cut at rehearsals. As I arranged the
production, the actor playing the Bishop did not come
on the stage as the Ghost of the dead Bishop in the
Forest scene in the last act. His silhouette—of
gigantic size—with uplifted arm appeared on the wall
of the set. This was effected by the actor standing
behind the flat, which represented the wall, and
which was made transparent by placing an arc lamp
behind him, projecting his shadow onto the flat. He
had to speak into a microphone so that his words
should not only be heard by the audience but also
sound very deep and " inhuman." At the start of the
scene the enthusiastic actor took his place, the arc
lamp went slowly up and he started to speak. I was
standing near and heard him begin the " cut " speech
and tried to stop him, but he paid no attention to me
and went on and on. As his long recitation muddled
all the cues of the following entrances I was obliged to
turn off the arc lamp and switch off the microphone,
much to his annoyance and bewilderment.

The play was produced in an enormous pavilion on

"The Tidings brought to Mary." The Scene in the Forest. N.Y. Theatre Guild, 1922. Komisarjevsky.

a cliff near the sea with seating for ten thousand people. The wind was so strong that the pavilion was blown down the first night it was put up, fortunately not during a performance. We had no proper stage and no front curtain, only a large platform on which we put a permanent set which I had designed, representing a combination of the royal Arms of Norway, and on which we fixed up a lighting installation of spots and arcs brought from London. The ends of the acts were intimated by the lights going out on the stage. I was warned before the performance that a Welsh audience can be very restless if it doesn't like a show and that then they usually start to sing, so at the beginning of our matinée both Lord Howard and myself were very nervous. (Lord Howard with his usual keenness and enthusiasm for everything concerning the real Theatre offered his services as stage manager, directed the music off stage and even beat the drums and turned the wind machines himself.) The sincerity and power of the actors took the audience. At the finale there was at first a long silence and then loud applause with shouts of " bravo " and even " bis," which lasted so long that we thought the audience would never leave unless we gave the whole play over again.

I think that the amateur movement in England and in the United States is already sufficiently strong and widespread to " threaten " the professional Theatre. I have seen amateur shows in the provinces of the

United States and England better acted and better produced than many an elaborate professional production in New York and London. It is possible that the " Renaissance of the Theatre " will come through the amateurs whose keenness, disinterestedness, unselfishness and sincerity is so necessary for the professional Theatre of to-day.

CHAPTER SEVEN

A conversation with a pupil—Teaching of acting—Acting on the commercial stage—Spiritual tradition and tradition of the routine— A young English actor—A young English actress—The " stars "— A play—A musical symphony—A bit of advice—An audition—My father's letter

IT happened in a " pub."

I like English pubs and English chemist shops. The London chemist shops are so bright and cheerful, especially at night, with their big glass bowls of coloured water in the windows. When I enter one of these shops, everything—medicines, tonics, perfumes —reminds me of radiant health, happiness and order. The London pub looks like a Continental chemist shop—more subdued and pedantic than the English one—and also reminds me of health, happiness, and order ; perhaps a purely imaginary health and happiness—but isn't it better to be able to imagine these things, than to feel ill or miserable ? In Sampierdarena—there is such a place in Italy—I once saw an inn, called : " Farmacia degli sani," and English pubs seem to me " chemist shops for healthy people."

I go to a chemist or a pub when lonely or miserable, but on leaving, I feel that life is really nothing but a matter of order, health and happiness, and if we are disorderly, ill and miserable, it's only because we don't want to cure ourselves.

Anyway, it was in a pub, a very respectable and artistic one. Over the mantelpiece hung a shield with the motto " Let conviviality be moderate and temperate," and on the walls were pictures of Garrick drinking the health of Goldsmith and Sir Joshua Reynolds " showing a portrait " to Mrs. Siddons, in which, however, the " portrait " seemed to be left entirely to the lady's imagination.

I entered that pub with a young man who was taking lessons with me—he wanted to learn to act, at any rate I had imagined up till then, that that was what he wanted of me. He had a whisky, which, as he said, was the " right thing to have at that time of day." I had a bitter. Encouraged by his drink my budding actor—he looked very " arty," with no hat, hair à la Henry Irving, tiepin and spats—addressed me as follows :

—Yesterday I saw some managers. I may get a job playing the part of (he named a part) in a No. 2 company which (he named a very good London actor) played in London.

—Hum—I said.

—A jolly good part, sir, a star part with every opportunity to act everyone else off the stage.

—Do you think you'll be able to act it ?

—If I didn't feel I could act that sort of part standing on my head, I shouldn't have gone on the stage—he replied with a smile, as if, he felt hurt it seemed to me, by my question.

—But you have only had five one hour lessons with me ?

—Yes, but I've got several useful hints from you. As a matter of fact, that's all I wanted.   I didn't tell you that I went through the course of the N. N. School of Drama and won a prize.

—I see—said I, remembering that the young man had very bad diction—why did you choose that school ?   Had you heard about the methods of teaching there and liked them ?

—No, sir.   They used to have a public show at the end of the last term, so I thought there would be a chance to be seen by managers.   You probably won't agree with me, but I think acting is a matter of personality and not of learning—and he stroked his hair with a nineteenth century ballet gesture and fingered his tie pin.

—Why did you come to me ?

—Because I admire your work.   Especially that production you did for Diaghileff's Russian Ballet.

—I've never produced anything for Diaghileff in my life, though I like his work very much.

—Didn't you ?   Of course not !   But you were with the Moscow Art Theatre, and I . . .

—I am sorry to disappoint you again, I was never with the Moscow Art Theatre, but never mind, tell me the real reason why you came to me ?

—Well, you are Russian and I've always heard

Russians are so clever, I thought you might give me some original ideas, some theatrical tricks unknown in this country. What is acting, after all, but a series of tricks!

—I have not shown you any tricks. I've told you already, I have no use for tricks.

—But you have!—He laughed—Watching you, I got lots of things which I'll be able to use, if I have to play a foreigner—and he gave me a bad imitation of some of my gestures and accent, much to the amazement of the barmaid and a gentleman in a sporting cap without a tie, who, it seemed to me, murmured under his alcoholic breath something about " These bloody foreigners ! "

—Let's sit down in a corner—said I, with a look at the gentleman minus neckwear.

Taking our drinks we went and sat under Mrs. Siddons admiring the blank portrait.

—Did you think it would be good publicity later for you to have had lessons from me ?—I asked him.

—Well,—he became a little embarrassed—if I have to play in a Russian play, then, yes, of course.

—Why only in a Russian ? The majority of the plays I have produced in my life have not been Russian. A producer, as well as an actor, must be a man of international culture. Art as well as science, is essentially international. It is in art and science that all nationalities meet on friendly terms and through art and science they understand each other and assist each other's development.   A great work of art is universal because of it's content and national because of its details.

—That's what you think on the Continent, sir, but we say that what's British is best, and ought to be done by the British. So I am afraid, sir,—he laughed apologetically—I shan't be able to use your name for publicity when playing in British plays. Besides, your ideas on acting and your methods of producing would be very good for us actors, if we had the time to learn them, and could have the pleasure of being produced by you, but from the point of view of the commercial stage where we have to earn our bread and butter, they are too highbrow and no use financially. You don't mind my saying this I hope?

—Of course not. I am glad to hear you speak frankly.

—Before coming to you—he went on, encouraged— I had some private lessons with a very old and experienced English variety actor, who calls himself Beethoven; he also gave me some very useful hints. He told me I had great talent for the stage.

—How much did you pay him?

—I don't remember exactly, but I think his fee was £20 for 10 lessons. He made a reduction on account of my ability, and charged me fifteen guineas for ten lessons. He found nothing wrong with me, except one little trouble, that I couldn't pronounce the " R's " and the " L's " and instead of saying " Kay " I said " Tay." So he made me recite with my mouth full of stones. He kept small round stones specially for that purpose.

—How interesting !

—Very ! Quite a revelation ! I believe in original methods and in combining all the different hints I have received from various people. The comedian taught me—he laughed apologetically—exactly the opposite to what you have told me. But if you don't mind my saying so, effects can be produced much more easily by his methods than by yours. For instance he told me never to look at a stage partner when speaking to him, because the audience would not then see my face. I have to look at my partner first, and then speak looking at the audience, and after finishing my speech look at him again ! Marvellous, isn't it ? He taught me some very good facial expressions and a lot of original " business." I know you told me that an expression ought only to appear on the face as the result of thoughts and feelings on the part of the character, and that stage " business " should be a sincere expression of what the character feels a desire to do. But you must admit that all that is quite unpractical for the modern stage. For instance, the manager who offered me the part, wanted me to read it to him and act it on the spot. How could I have done that with your " system ? "

—Were you acquainted with the play beforehand ?

—I had never heard of it !

—In that case I don't think you could have done it

COSTUMES FOR "COSI FAN TUTTE." Komisarjevsky.

properly with any system. Besides, no one can judge an actor from a first reading, or even from the first few rehearsals. The part must sink into an actor's mind before he can really act it. He must " find himself in the part " before he can perform it sincerely and originally. I know of good actors who have been kicked out of a caste by impatient producers merely because they were slow while rehearsing. Some of those actors played the same parts very well later, when produced by other people, or left to themselves.

—But to work in the commercial Theatre—he continued—one must be quick, sir, and an actor must possess a permanent stock of expressions gestures and inflections. He offered me a Gold Flake. The commercial actor must think first of all of his commercial success, and so he must use all the traditional and well tested stock expressions and tricks which have already met with success with managers as well as the public. Besides, why should I rack my brains to discover some new way of acting a part when the man producing the show can tell me exactly how to do it or how it was done by some famous actor who made a big hit in it ?

—I am afraid you underrate the intelligence of the public. They are already getting sick and tired of those " rubber stamps " which every mediocre actor uses.

—I love originality, sir, but believe me, I can't try original and as you call it " sincere " acting on audiences without running the risk of being out of a job.

The public want to see again and again what they have liked before.   My comedian was so useful because he knew exactly what is wanted for the commercial stage, and could show me how to get big effects without too much work or trouble.   By the way, he wrote a very good book for young actors in which he describes everything we really need, not only facial expressions and gestures for various circumstances, but also exactly how to act people in different states of mind, such as " hunger," " thirst," " egotism," " pride," " sensuality," " gambling agitation," " love to one's neighbour," " sexual love," " illness," and even " death ! "

At this I could not help smiling.

—Have you never seen that book ?

—No.

—It's marvellous !   He spent half his life writing it from personal experience of the traditions of other actors.

—Do you know that Rossi said . . .

—Who ?

—Rossi, one of the greatest actors.

—Never heard of that Russian.

—He was an Italian.   In his book " Studii Dramatici " Rossi says that an actor must first cultivate his mind and that imitating other actors, however great they may be, does not help but hinders.   He said there were two kinds of " tradition," the spiritual one, which tells us how the analysis of a part was made by a great actor, and the tradition of routine, which is a

soulless repetition by generations of actors of the
means of expression of some great actors.   He says
that the spiritual tradition should be studied but not
be accepted if the actor's own feeling and judgment of
the part doesn't coincide with it.   One actor should
not fall into the sin of imitating another actor.   The
voice, gestures, inflections and the gradations of
feeling of each actor—in a word the whole interpretation of a part—must always be his own.   Mere
imitation reduces the Theatre to the level of a school of
apes or monkeyism, " scimmiottamento " as Rossi
called it.

—But that actor of yours was a foreigner!—retorted
my young friend. What he said may be all right for his
own country, but here when a manager asks me to
read a part on the spot, I can't tell him I must study it
first, as there are about fifty people waiting on the
stairs outside to get it !   Luckily, as well as being able
to " make tears come out of my left eye " when he
told me to, I was the right type.   One must *look* the
part to-day, sir, and if one has a voice as well, and
knows some tricks—well—anyone can do it !   No one
wants any other sort of " acting " nowadays !   I was
told when still at school that I was the right type to
play leads, and you'll see, I shall play them !   It is not
the same in England as in your country, where girls
of twenty play old women, and women of forty young
girls.   I never could understand how they do it and
I must say I am not sufficiently interested to try to
find out.

—What made you go on the stage? Excessive vanity?

—Well, every actor must be ambitious, mustn't he? I love the stage, and . . .

—No one can really love or hate what he knows nothing about, especially in the arts. Nessuna cosa si puo amare ne odiare—said Leonardo da Vinci—se prima non si ha cognition di quella. Read this—and I took a letter from my pocket and showed him the following passage :

—" I often wonder what on earth induced the people with whom I am now playing to go on the stage ! If I asked them they would probably reply that it was ' love of the Theatre,' but that's a lie ! I don't think nine actors or actresses out of ten know why they went on the stage. The majority of them probably had the semiconscious desire to become famous somehow and found that they got more limelight by going on the stage than they could ever have had in any other occupation. They had probably heard and read in the papers of actors surrounded by crowds of admirers. They saw the chance of becoming quite important and unique people, and finally vanity pushed them into the Theatre. I also think some kind of sexual and psychological perversity—the desire to exhibit themselves bodily, and a neurotic desire to put " le coeur a nu "—often has something to do with the longing to go on the stage. We have with us a young actress the shyest and most prudish creature in ordinary life, but on the stage she has no objection to showing her legs as far up as where they begin, and she can act the most passionate scenes in the most realistic seductive way.   You would say it was necessary to the part.   I know it is.   But what surprised me is the pleasure she gets out of doing it, not as the character she is playing, but as herself.   Another young actress here is probably so accustomed to such exhibitions, that she has lost all bodily sensitiveness . . .

—Who wrote that ?

—A young man now on tour.

—One of those unsuccessful actors who find fault with everything and everybody but themselves !—He handed me the letter, but I showed him another passage in it :

— . . . " I have been three years on the stage and I see that the Theatre is crowded with people who have nothing in them whatever to justify their desire to be actors or actresses.   Not only are they complete ignoramuses as regards the most elementary things in their profession, but they lack the very fundamentals of histrionic talent . . ."

—He exaggerates of course, but there is some truth in what he says about the overcrowding of the stage. The dickens only knows how they manage to get jobs and to push people out who *can* act !

—If it were not for that competition you would be playing leads in town, and not in a No. 2 company on tour—said I, searching my pockets, which serve me as office files.

—Yes, of course—said he getting up—have another ?

—No thank you.

—I will—and he went to fetch his drink.

When he returned I gave him another letter.

—This is from a talented girl of eighteen who is playing a lead on tour in a No. 1 company at £6 a week.

He put the letter to his nose.

—Nice smell !—he remarked and then read :

—" I have to act my strenuous part in this town twice daily, and I am so worn out that I no longer know what I am doing while on the stage. I cry every night while eating the cheese and salad my landlady gives me for supper. I cry in bed which feels like a hammock made of barbed wire. I cry in my dressing-room before every show and only wipe my tears away to put the make up on. When at school I was told by my teachers, and I knew it myself, that I could act, and I loved thinking of my future and of studying acting. But now I hate my work, which has nothing to do with the art of acting, it's only a stupid pretence, a bluff and mere slavery ! I know I am a good actress, and that makes me hate my present work all the more, because it is gradually killing all the talent I ever had. I've been told I have no sense of humour . . ." Quite right too ! She ought to have a sense of humour !—Remarked my friend.

—" And I am rather glad of it, if having any, means being ashamed of and laughing at everything one sin-

cerely feels. I don't want to laugh at what I feel about
my acting. As I realise the difference between the job I
have got and the real work of an actress, I refuse to become, like many others, indifferent to what they do and
how they do it, so long as they get their money every
week and satisfy their desire to feel important. When I
was given my present part I worked hard on it by myself before rehearsals, though I never saw the script of
the play.   Three days before the first rehearsal I was
presented with what is called a " part "—my lines
typewritten between short meaningless cues.   At
rehearsals the producer wouldn't let me do anything I
had thought of myself, not because he had anything
more interesting to show me, but because the part had
already been played in town by another actress whom
he wanted me to imitate.   He showed me all her
movements and inflections and insisted on my repeating
them like a parrot, and pooh poohed all my own ideas."
    —The girl thinks too much, that's the trouble !   A
highbrow !   There are producers and authors to
think for actors!—Remarked my friend and went on
reading :
    —" At each rehearsal I felt I was getting worse and
worse, more and more self-conscious and tied up—
and at last I became like a block of wood and lost all
confidence . . ."
    —She should have been jolly glad that he took all
that trouble with her !   What are producers for if not
to show gestures and inflections ?   Where was I ?
Yes, that's it :—" a block of wood " . . .

—" The dresses they have made for me are simply awful, and I am conscious of them all the time and feel neither myself nor the character of my part. You know what appearance means to an actor and especially to a woman . . ."

—That's more a dressmaker's business—mumbled he, turning the page of the letter :

—" We have a girl in our company (he read the name of the girl) . . .

—I saw her acting with amateurs—said I—and she was a very good " Shrew."

—Shakespeare !—exclaimed my friend—muck ! So dull, bores me stiff ! West End managers fight shy of Shakespearean actors—they're always out of work, and one of our critics said that Shakespeare is the tomb of talent.

—Really !—said I.

—Yes. The only sort of Shakespeare I can stand is when it's in " modern dress," as it's been done in London a few times the last few years. Don't you agree ?

—I do not. Hamlet in plus fours or Macbeth in khaki uniform cannot sound or look otherwise than a skit, a parody. The poetical form and style of Shakespeare's plays may belong to all ages, and he may be (I think that he even *should* be) produced in a conditional poetical theatrical form belonging to *all* ages, but neither the form nor the style of Shakespeare's plays have anything to do with " modern " dress or modern environment.

—Well, even if these productions are no better than skits they have an advantage over the " stock " ones, they're not so hopelessly dull.   What is the Theatre, after all, but an amusement ?   An American writer who visited our School of Dramatic Art said that the English Theatre was a huge joke.   He meant it nastily, of course, but I don't think he could have paid a better compliment to our Theatre.

He had another sip at his drink and again took up the letter.

—" She can act, but she couldn't get a job in London, because they said she wasn't the type . . ."

—There you see !—exclaimed he triumphantly.

—" She neither looks like a vamp nor an insipid ingenue. . . . She has now given up all hopes on the stage and is going to marry a rich American . . ."

—Jolly good too !

—" My disappointment "—continued my friend, skipping a few lines—" in the stage began with my first engagement a year ago, when I played in a two weeks' *try out* of a play which never reached town.   The production was the same sort of thing as my present one.   Although my part had never been played before, I was obliged to mimic the producer and be nothing but an automaton for telling the story of the play.   During the first week, in Blackpool, it was hell.   Although we had been rehearsing twice daily without salary for four weeks in town, they made us rehearse every day in Blackpool while playing at night.   The first dress rehearsal on a

Sunday lasted from five p.m., until two a.m., and the second on Monday, the night we opened, from eleven a.m., until three p.m. All this—what for? To improve our acting? To better the team work? Not at all. Only to get more realism into a thunder storm in the second act (which by the way, never came off properly) and in order to juggle with the play at the last moment, transposing scenes and altering lines to (as they said) make a success of it, but they really only succeeded in muddling and confusing everyone. The producer of that play was not so obstinate as the one who produced the one I am in now. After putting me completely off my idea of the part by the end of the rehearsals, he agreed that after all, the reading I had given at the first rehearsal without his help was the better, and told me to play the part as I wanted to . . ."

He again skipped some lines :

—" . . . I'm not going to give up the stage. I shall go on acting as they want me to, but I won't allow the real talent that is in me to die,and when the time comes, I'll show them ! I'll become a star, famous and independent, and then I will act as the artist in me tells me to act . . ."

—Every young actor's ambition should be to become a " star."—He handed me the letter—I'll work my way to stardom too !—He added leaning back and putting his hands in his trouser pockets.

—I am glad you have so much faith in yourself. An actor needs it ! Besides, once a star, you'll have plenty of opportunity " to act everybody else off the stage," as you said.

He looked at me with a smile.

—Are you making fun of me ?

—Why should I ?   A star-actor, as *you* use the word, always does so or tries to.

—What do you mean by " as you use the word star ? "

—I'll have another bitter.—Said I, getting up and trying to change the conversation.

—Can I get it for you ?

—No, thank you.

I came back and my young friend then asked me :

—Have you heard of . . . ? (He named a star actor-manager now dead)   His secretary, a jolly good producer now—when he can get something to produce, that is—told me lots of stories about him.   Do you know, he wouldn't touch a play if there were another really good part in it besides his own, or even if there were a good part for a woman.   He never engaged a really good actor in his company lest he should overshadow him.   When rehearsing, he would never allow anyone else to " take the stage," mask him, or be up stage.   I heard two marvellous stories about him.   Once he had to play a scene with another man who came on down stage, when he himself, of course, was in the centre and up stage. The actor who had entered, seeing he would have to play with his back to the audience, moved up stage till he was level with the star.   Then the latter, being

o

obliged to play with his profile to the audience instead
of facing it, moved a step up stage, so as to face the
audience.   Whereupon the other, noticing this, also
took a step up stage.   The star of course retreated
another step, and so they kept on walking step by
step up stage, until they came up against the back of
the set!   Ha-ha-ha-ha!   You can imagine what a
row the star kicked up afterwards!   On another
occasion this star noticed that one of his partners
always got a round after a certain speech, and one
night when he finished the line leading to that speech,
quickly added : " I know, what you want to tell me "
and spoke the successful speech himself and got the
round!   Very clever, wasn't it ?   But he was really a
bit too selfish!   He once gave a young actor the sack
because the chap got all the notices.   One of the
critics had been so inconsiderate as to advise the star
to learn how to move on the stage from that young
man.   Of course, one can't altogether blame the
star from getting rid of the young actor, but still . . . !
Fancy saying a thing like that about a man with a
reputation!   After that the star wouldn't let the
critic in to his next first night!   It was very plucky of
him, don't you think ?

As I didn't reply he asked me :

—You didn't tell me what you meant by my use of
the word " star ? "   How many kinds of star are there
then ?

—Well, you see—said I—there has never been a
play written for what *you* call " star " acting.   Every

play is like a musical symphony, in which the " whole " matters above all else.   The actors are like voices in the orchestra, which forms the harmony of the piece. Sometimes one predominates, sometime another, but the right balance of the whole, its form, rhythm, and time, is always maintained. 'A play is written with the idea of producing certain reactions on the audience by its action.   The actions of the single characters, dependent upon one another, together form a series of continuous patterns.   Those patterns, moving in a definite rhythm and changing their shapes as in a kaleidoscope, one pattern blending into the next one, represent the action of the whole play.   If you take the action of one character out of a play, or under or over emphasise it, the action of the whole play is disjuncted.   Every adaptation of a play to the requirements of a selfish actor, or producer, for the purpose of making of it a suitable " acting or producing vehicle," is equivalent to the murder of a play. " King Lear," " Hamlet," " Othello " are very fine acting parts, but by no means for " star " actors whose main ambition is to show the public what tricks they have in their theatrical " boxes " or to exhibit no matter by what means, the most attractive aspects of their vain personalities, even if so doing involves annihilating everyone in the play, including the author himself.   One cannot conceive the part of Othello without his relationship with Iago, Desdemona Cassio and the other characters, and the *better* those parts are played, all the better for a good actor in the

part of Othello.   A good painter wouldn't like to
have figures painted on his canvas by some other bad
painter !   Every scene in a play is an ensemble in
which one actor stimulates the words and actions of
another by his own, in which one actor by words and
actions gives depth, light and shade to the words and
actions of another.   When a scene is acted harmoniously and rhythmically, everyone participating in it
creates the atmosphere, which makes the audience
" live " with the scene.   This is as it should be, instead of the attention of the audience being rivetted to
one person only or divided between different actors,
or watching alternately an exhibition of personalities
and tricks.   There can never be an actor great
enough to enable an audience to overlook the bad
acting of his " supporters " and capable of interpreting
a whole play by himself.   The scenes in " Othello "
in which the principal actor does not appear are
as important for the balance and atmosphere of the
tragedy as those in which the audience sees him.
The tragic climax in the acting of the principal actor
in the storm scenes in " King Lear " would never be
felt by the audience as strongly as it should be if
Goneril and Regan were not played in the preceding
scenes on the same gigantic scale as Lear himself, and
if the actions of every character in the play did not
lead to that climax through different well balanced
conflicts between them and Lear.   The great human
meaning of Shakespeare's tragedy, signified by a
struggle between the earthly powers of good and

"FATA MALERBA." The second act. Komisarjevsky.

evil, in which " good " goes down to suffering, folly
and death, could not be made clear and impressive
on the stage unless in the storm scenes Lear and the
Fool play as in a harmonious duet, followed by the
trio Kent, Lear and the Fool, which is joined by
Edgar, thus forming a quartette. Lear, the Fool,
Edgar and Kent complete each other in those scenes
and once together form one single gigantic character.
Facing in their agonies, " the wrathful skies," the
" spouting of cataracts and hurricanes," and the " all
shaking thunder," sent by merciless Gods to strip
them and make them see their own souls, they are all
of equal value for that scene, and for the idea of the
play. The storm itself, symbolising " the tempest
raging in their minds," is a rhythmical accompaniment
to their acting, accentuating its " forte's " and "piano"
and following its transitions. The parts of Lear,
Othello, Hamlet, etc., are by themselves only frag-
ments of a work of art and they could only be played
by first rate artists, who know what theatrical interpretation and team work means, and who know how
to act rhythmically with their partners and to subordin-
ate themselves to the requirements of a scene as a
whole. The work of a leading actor in these plays
should be compared not to the playing of a soloist
who stands in front of the orchestra, while the latter
accompanies him, but to the playing of a big part in a
symphony by a very good musician, sitting in the
orchestra itself. Some parts have been written or
arranged by authors—as, for example, Magda in

Sudermann's play and Nora in the " Doll's House "
to suit the methods of acting of certain actors and
actresses.   But even those plays were not written
to suit *your* ideas of " star acting."   In the first
place the actresses whom Sudermann and Ibsen
had conceived in the parts of Magda and Nora were
sound versatile actresses and not mediocrities who
needed specially concocted parts in which to display
their poor acting abilities.   Secondly, there are other
good parts in those plays besides Magda and Nora,
and the interpretation of the latter in " Heimath "
and " The Doll's House " depends as in any other
play, on the ensemble.   Two of the greatest moments
of Duse's acting in " The Doll's House " were—when
she was saying Nora's line in the last act :—" I thank
you for your forgiveness," and when she listened to
Torwald's speech before saying that line.   She did
not draw the public's attention to herself while
listening to the long speech of Torwald, as *your* " star "
would do, but focussed it on the speaker by her quiet
demeanour while watching him.   She knew that
unless she gave full scope to the words and actions of
her partner her reply would lack meaning.   She
knew the importance of team work in acting,
though she could not always afford a company of
good actors when touring.

—So you think there should be no stars on the
stage at all?—asked my future actor, finishing his
second drink.

—There should certainly be no stars of *your* kind,

but as there are some plays in which the ensemble
dominates, there are others in which one, two, or
three actors dominate, and leading actors must
always exist.   Besides, great actors will always
dominate others and must have outstanding rôles
to afford them the material to show their talent.   It is
true that great actors make even small parts seem
great.   Tiberio Fiorilli as Scaramouche acted a scene
without words catching a fly for a couple of minutes,
and the interest of the audience did not drop.   But
it is also true that acting good parts helps an actor
to expand his talent.   The fact is that a leading actor
or a " star," or whatever you call him, must have
enough of the artist in him to understand a play as a
whole and to know that the production of any play
is based on a well balanced ensemble of all its
elements.

I looked at my friend who remained silent, either
thinking of what I had just said or listening to the
wireless which had been put on by the proprietor of the
pub, which I have already said was a very artistic
one.

A woman's voice, coming out of a black megaphone
over the bar, sang :

" Are you lonesome to-night,
Do you miss me to-night ? "

Then something I couldn't hear, and then :—

" Does your memory stray
To a bright summer's day,
When I kissed you
And called you swee-ee-eet heart ! "

—Let me give you a bit of advice—said I touching the budding actor's arm.

—Certainly, I shall be obliged.

—If you want to become *somebody* on the stage, work.   Work hard and don't get desperate.

—I'll never lose my nerve.   I have enough sense of humour—answered he.

—It's a good thing to have a sense of humour, but don't have too much.   Remember that a temporary success with the public or the press doesn't mean anything.   You may fit the part or the part may fit you.   You may be the " right type," or you may on one occasion succeed in bringing off a good, life-like hysterical fit, or a clever imitation of a certain accent, or in simulating a " character " with the aid of a couple of borrowed grimaces and gestures—and people will proclaim you marvellous, great or even the " best actor on the British Stage."   That happens often nowadays.   If you put any faith in these hymns of praise you will fall from your pedestal as quickly as you were placed there.   The same people will gladly throw you down with the same eagerness.   *Real* success comes neither quickly nor easily, as it is the result of strenuous training, of long self-criticism, of a deep knowledge of yourself and many other things.

ENGLISH COMMERCIAL THEATRICAL POSTER

Start with small parts, imagine that each of them is a wonderful part, and make them into good parts by your acting. Enjoy acting, but don't forget that it is training you at the same time. Don't try above all " to be a success," but think of the meaning of what you say and do on the stage. Try to improve at every performance the sincerity of your acting and the conception of the character. Remember that there was never a great actor who became great all at once, and that there was never a great actor who was old in his mind and traditional in his acting. All great actors have been daring people who fought the old " schools " and routine for the sake of new ideas. And my last advice is :—give up the stage, run away from it, as soon as you see that you will never be any better than hundreds of others.

—Ye-es—said he, lighting a cigarette.
The woman on the wireless still sang :

" Do you gaze at your do-o-or step
    And picture me there ?"

—Now I must go. I have a rehearsal.—I got up and shook hands—Good luck. Have you signed your contract yet ?
—Not yet.
When we came out into the street, he suddenly turned to me :
—There will be a leading lady in the company too. Of course she will be starred on the bills. Don't you

think I ought to insist on having my name put at the bottom of the cast :—" *and* So and So ? "

—Do you know a story about Tree. A girl once came up to him after an audition and said :—Mother says, sir, that if I am to play this part my name must be put after yours : " Herbert Tree *and* Miss Smith," to which Tree replied : " Why not *but*, my dear young lady ? "

The future actor laughed strangely.

—Good bye, sir—said he after a short pause.— Many thanks !—and he rushed away.

*   *   *   *

My company had not yet arrived when I reached the rehearsal rooms, but the room was full of people. Some management was holding an audition, a try out of an ingenue understudy for a musical comedy—I was told.   A girl frantically twisting her long thin bare legs in short black knickers and shaking under a patchy sleeveless blouse, was performing in a corner, and a tiny old woman jumping up and down in her chair was mercilessly hitting an upright piano. A bored looking man in shirt sleeves with a cigar in his mouth was sitting in the middle of the room on the only chair besides that of the pianist.   It was the producer.   Near him was the agent.   In another corner of the room was a crowd of semi-undressed actresses, some sitting on the floor, waiting their turn.

—Thank you, miss !—Shouted the producer.

The girl in the patchy blouse breathing heavily, made an awkward bow and joined the crowd in the corner.

—Next please, Miss John !—Called the agent.

A smartly dressed girl in a tailor-made costume stepped forward and began a song with " business " and dance steps.

—Lift your skirts, Miss, let me see your legs. Higher please, miss !—Said the producer in an indifferent voice.

The smart girl did as she was ordered.

—Thank you, Miss John.   You'll hear from us.— He whispered to the agent :—No good—the knees stick out !

—Next please.

A woman of about fifty took her place. She danced and sang with a fixed smile and trying hard to be a young girl, but all the same anxiety of being out of work again was stamped on her features.

—Thank you, Miss—er-er !

The woman stopped her exhibition and looked appealingly at the producer.

—You'll hear from us.   Next please—and another elderly lady stepped forward.

It was rather close in the room and I went into the passage ; I saw a girl there, probably a secretary, taking the names of all those who passed, but not putting down their addresses.   A few minutes later the agent came out into the passage.

—We are through !   Sheer waste of time !   We've

seen sixty of 'em—all rotten. Yesterday I had to choose the crowd for a film, and out of two hundred I got fifty.

—How many film actors are there in London?—I asked him.

—How many?   Half London!

—How many theatrical ones?

—Enough for twenty times as many Theatres as there are.

I went to the window. The sun was shining. I still heard in my ears the voice from the wireless:

> " Does your memory stray
> To a bright summer day . . ."

I thought of my father, who, after 35 years work on the stage and for the stage, went to live on a farm in Italy, from where he wrote to my sister :—

" You are standing on the banks of a stagnant and stinking pond and you suffer because it is never drained. You are enthusiastic about your work but you forget the simple truth that the theatrical pool has existed for centuries and that only a few are chosen for the arduous task of draining the theatrical dyke. You ought to have known beforehand that you would not be exactly happy doing the work you had undertaken and that you would never see the results of it yourself . . . You have the choice of two things :— rich meals in the company of a pack of gluttons, or, as the result of sincere work, which in itself will raise against you a host of opportunists who thrive in the stagnation of the theatrical quagmire—a solitude in which you will often go hungry and a road through life which does not lead along the path of enjoyment but of unhappiness. If you feel unable to make the sacrifice, you must either leave the stage or make up your mind to join the ranks of the servants of Mammon."

THE END